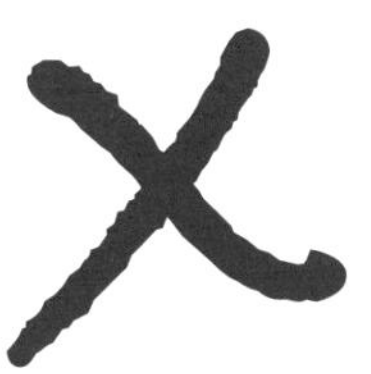

THE ICE PLANT • 2026

Isn't

X

Beautiful!

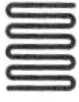

Odette Elix England

ALSO BY ODETTE ELIX ENGLAND

To Be Developed, To Be Continued

The Long Shadow:
Unwrapped ~ Marion Post Wolcott's Labor and Love

Woman Wearing Ring Shields Face from Flash

Past Paper // Present Marks (with Jennifer Garza-Cuen)

Dairy Character

Keeper of the Hearth:
Picturing Roland Barthes' Unseen Photograph

CHAPTERS

I   Overlooking

II   They call it Xanadu

III   Cross your legs, say cheese!

IV   Noxious

V   P.S. I expect these xxxoooxxx

VI   Good and bad things come in threes

VII   Black and white and red (and brown and blue) all over

VIII   Xanax, pissing about

IX   Null-forgiving operator

X   Exodus

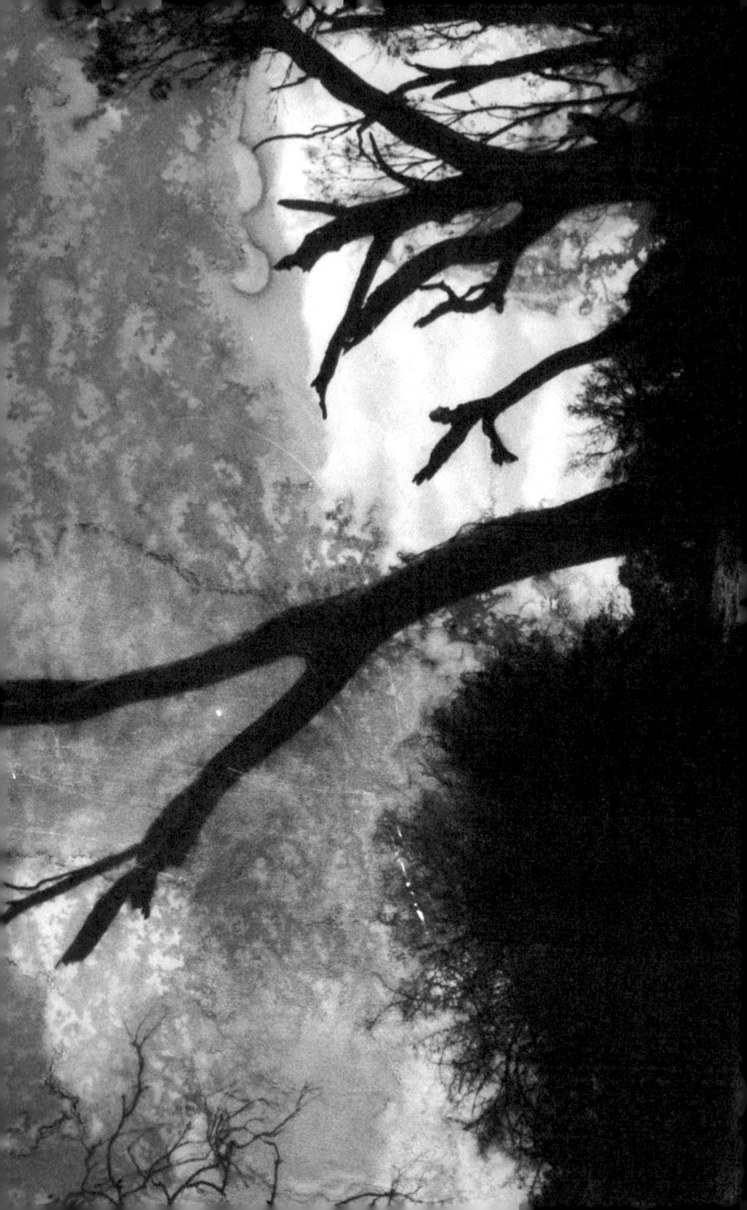

I

Overlooking

This is how I learned about photography. And bodies.

Dad carves an uppercase X into the thirsty dirt with his rubber-boot-clad right foot. Sunlight floats the dust aloft. Grunts of frustration clash with the nippy air. He curses and shoves the greasy calf to his left.

Spring is calving season, which means photography season. Frontal, flagrant, in-your-face photography. The calves in the holding pen dash to the fence and thrust their heads at the cyclone wire, pushing forward their fatty pink-ish-grayish tongues. They love to lick things and love to be licked. I let them saturate my arms in gluey slobber. It feels weird but nice.

This X-marks-the-spot spot for photograph-ing calves is on the east side of Dad's dairy, in front of the rusted railings overlooking the corral, runoff, and segments of bank-owned acreage—low paddocks, even lower paddocks, the sunken once-upon-a-time-were paddocks—all leading to the swamps skirting the river.

Dad persists in coercing feisty calves to ten-hut. He wrangles a body into position and steps back. Spits, clicks, and pulls the film tab, *shk-shk*, like the sound of a credit card imprinter. He slips the picture into his pocket, rests his Polaroid SX-70 camera atop an engine oil drum, and steers the photographed body back to the pen. You're up, Bessie, Flossie, Missy, no, not you, dumbass. He's got a black marker behind his right ear to check-mark the back of the photograph (yes) or X the front (fucked up). A permanent mark, the kind that haunts farmers' wives and their worn hands. After ten clicks and many shit-bugger-pisses, he tosses the empty film cartridge for us kids to fight over. Brother BJ is quick, but I am strong and grab the cartridge to use as my pretend camera for the rest of the day, saying *click* out loud like a doofus.

I didn't know then that I was an image waiting to develop.

To the west of Dad's dairy are three gum trees too stringy to climb but perfect for stripping bark in the hope of finding spiders to torment with a stick. The first tree is the scraggiest, its branches extending to the southeast, along which metal meat hooks hang cold and bloody. Farmers' wind chimes, they call them. Where the boys dangle and dry out, for only female calves are worthy of photography. Today, under the skylark-song-blue sky, three bulls hang upside down, hemorrhaging into the dirt, their inky black bodies swaying, skulls knocking in the wind. Hundreds of bull ants congregate below, sucking up the blood. Each rump is marked with an X spray-painted in ready-for-market red. X for male, X for axed. It's as glossy and messy a memory now as it was then.

Typing at Mum's kitchen table, I'm listening to a recording of the photographer Collier Schorr talking about how we're born into a culture of bodies and that we see other bodies through our own. That we can't invent a body from scratch, but we can reinvent one with the camera. That nostalgia blocks things. That pictures of yesterday are boring. That documentary photography is predatory. That all the pictures already exist. All these 'thats' make me wonder about a type of photography I'll call 'hindsight photography,' when we take pictures in moments of reflection or regret. When we look at our younger selves in flat form and wish we could go back and give one piece of advice. I'd tell her (me): *When you grow up, you'll want to be a kid.*

I overlooked many things at our farm, like collecting Dad's X-marked Polaroids before he chucked them in the fireplace. The should-have-taken-a-picture pictures: dead rabbits and snake skins we hid in Mum's laundry to scare the bejesus out of her; the strange weather balloon we found that time; the nooks and crannies of Dad's barn where wild feelings caught fire. Mental pictures I wish I could forget: my parents' first fight (the first time I saw Mum cry) or when I roped myself to a fence in protest upon learning our farm was for sale. Pictures we had, but no one could find, like the one of my first black eye.

When Nietzsche wrote about the eye outside of time and history, I like to think he was talking about a camera.

The Automatic 100 Land camera, introduced by the Polaroid Corporation in 1963 and named for its co-founder, the inventor Edwin Land, was the first to use pack film. Nine years later came the SX-70, a folding single-lens reflex camera, the SX meaning 'Special eXperiment.' Both cameras are gifts to Dad from Old Jack Adams across the field. He tells Dad there are no more pictures to look forward to.

Mum has a Kodak Instamatic X-45, one of many cameras with an X in its name. Online forums offer theories about what each X stands for, something to do with speed, time, or multiplication. Kodak Double X is two times the standard film speed of 100. Kodak Tri-X is three times the standard. Kodak Plus X is a bit faster than the standard. But X feels too iconic to be a standard of anything. And we don't have free will to choose our icons, says Collier Schorr.

I've photographed our former farm for about twenty-one years. There's one road in and out. That road, my primer to place, is my way-back machine.

Our farm has changed hands eight times since we left. When something changes hands, ownership transfers. There's an exchange, a handshake, an expiry date, a cooling off, and then a point of no return. I remember Dad signing on the dotted line next to the X, Mum leaning over Dad's shoulder, blowing her warm breath to help speed-dry the black ink on the contract of sale. Like a magic trick without magic. *Poof!* Our farm disappeared.

Whenever I go back, I knock on the door and ask permission. *I lived here X years ago. I've been returning for X years to take photographs, see? Can I walk around and take some more?* (How to walk around a photograph?) *I won't get in your way; cross my heart and hope to die.* But my heart already feels wronged and wrung out, and my hope is to reincarnate as an axolotl, the only creature that can regrow missing body parts if they are damaged, even the brain and heart.

Our farm is an ex I cannot, will not, give up. Put out to pasture before her prime, before her body was emptied of use. I've buried my negatives and photographs in her depths for years, depositing times passed, never marking the ground with an X with my size eleven feet. If I'm going to talk about memory and walk about memory, depress upon the dirt and the pity of dust-to-dust, I must be faithful to the mind and the mind's eye.

I forget where I bury them. They become tombs for amnesia.

Very few photographs I make at our farm come fast. Fewer still come into sharp focus. I ask myself why I can't make this photograph be what I want it to be. *This photograph* doesn't want to be a photograph. She wants to be another story in another body, a drifter who doesn't want to exist in an altered state—a beautiful object amongst objects. When I touch our farm with my eyes, she touches my whole body. *This photograph* has no interest in the speed or time of death.

The photographer Sophie Calle once said that the most beautiful things about the countryside are written in the city. Dad spits. No shit, city folk see the glory, no guts. Mum suggests that I let it lie. I extend the word *lie* until there's hardly any air in my lungs. Mum makes that face she makes. It's one of many semi-dramatic scenes repeatedly played at her kitchen table.

I can't let it lie. I can't get over looking.

Curiosity leads me to Dad's garage. I want to open the twenty-three still-unpacked heavy-duty archive boxes from our farm. I imagine nesting dolls of curses spilling from them. Dad warns me: it's a big loose thread of motherfuckers, don't do it. But if you do, wear a sweater, says Mum. It's as cold as death in there.

Colder, getting colder, colder now, you're freezing! Brother BJ and I loved to play Hot and Cold. The adult version is exasperating: when you're in one of those push-pull, on-off relation-ships that toy with your ideas of nearness and farness—a modern weapon for manipulating the psyche. I've been in that relationship with our farm since 1989. And I am the perp, keeping it cool, keeping my distance, all the while keeping in touch.

'Censor the body, and you censor breath and speech at the same time,' writes Hélène Cixous in "The Laugh of the Medusa." 'Write yourself. Your body must be heard.' I am a firewalker, a seashell to my ear. I go back to the embers of our farm because the dark souls of nostalgia cannot be expelled from my soles or camera.

I will make *this photograph*.

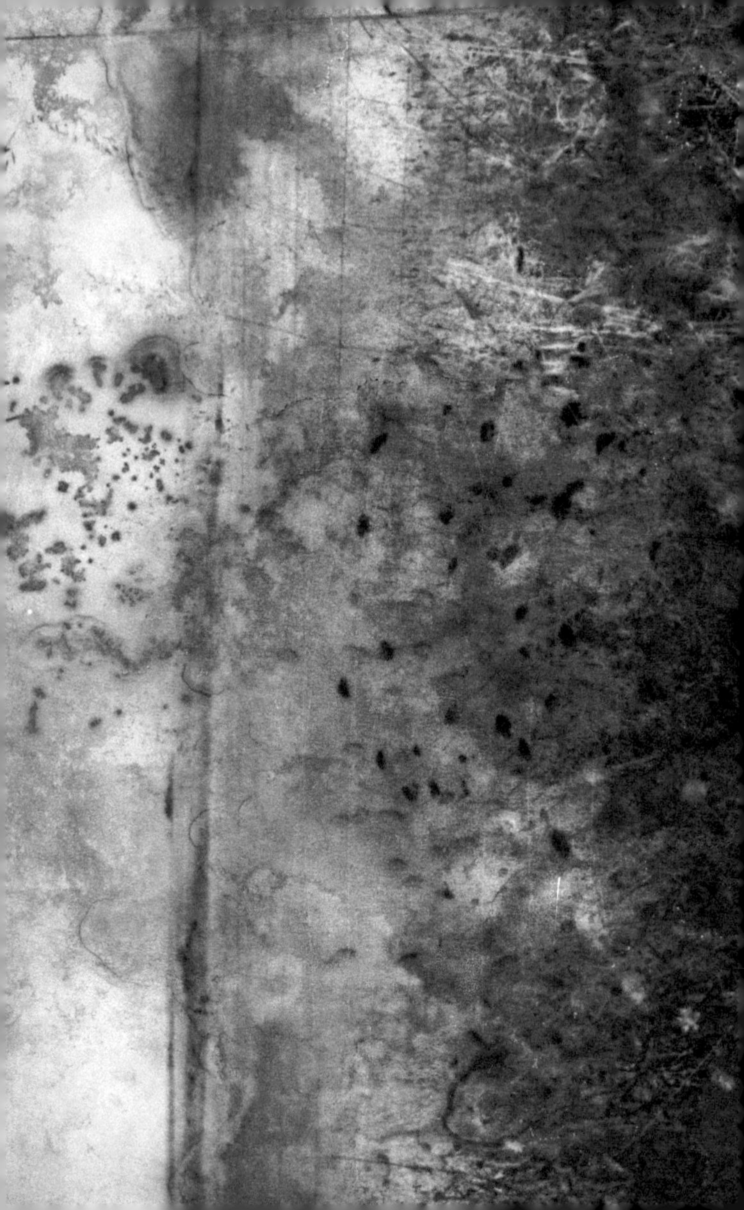

II

They call it Xanadu

A place where nobody dared to go
The love that we came to know
They call it Xanadu
(it takes your breath,
and it'll leave you blind)

—Jeff Lynne, "Xanadu" (1980)

I'm a proud Gen Xer, born in 1975, the same year Steven Sasson invented the world's first digital camera. Sasson's employer, Eastman Kodak, wasn't keen on his eight-pound camera, which took 0.01-megapixel black-and-white photos and recorded them onto cassette tape. Each image took twenty-three seconds to process, and the only way to view them was on a standard television screen.

NO PHOTOGRAPHS ALLOWED, it says on the maternity ward door. Soon-to-be fathers are also forbidden. Auntie Sylvia is the midwife on duty. At 5:25am, before Dad finishes milking the cows, his newborn eight-pounder is displayed behind glass. Auntie Sylvia scrawls Baby X on an index card above my crib and swoons. Isn't X beautiful! I'm handed to Old Mrs. Evans, the landowner's wife, the next day. She looks after me while Mum tucks her post-birth body into a spare pair of Old Jack Adams's overalls to help rake cow shit for the vegetable garden.

I try to imagine myself as a camera and realize I've been one since opening my eyes.

My surname, Elix, is tricky to pair. Mum wants to call me Mary Ann, but my cousin is Sharon Ann, and we ain't no copycats, declares

Dad. He thumbs the baby names book he uses for his calves. Lynx, Magnitude, Nazareth, Peaches, Quack. He settles on Odette, which means lover of home. A gift and an omen.

Elix has Prussian roots. In RGB color space, hex #003153, also known as Prussian blue, is composed of zero percent red, 19.2 percent green, and 32.5 percent blue. Every day before breakfast, Mum interprets the sky from her kitchen window: hopeless-blue, rainy-day-blue, fuming-blue, big-storm-blue, midwinter-blue. Always weather or emotion blue. Blue is blue, woman! Mum disagrees with Dad in a way so subtle I wonder *how to photograph a hint of disappointment.*

Xanadu is a color, too. RGB 115 134 120, the muddy gum-tree green of Mum's bathroom tiles.

No one else in our farming community has an X in their last name. The older locals are suspicious about what the X stands for. Dad says they're wary of things they find strange, like the long-standing rumor about a body buried under the old telephone box southeast of Old Tony Kenny's upper paddock. When the phone company removes the box, they exhume the partial skeleton of an adult male, identity and age unknown. No one speaks ill of our surname or mentions the phone box again. Whenever I return, I lay a bunch of *Oenothera biennis* at the site. Each flower has four Xanthic petals (RGB 238, 237, 9) and an X-shaped stigma. They smell like lemons but also superphosphate, peppercorns, and diesel, all in the air there.

You doodled them in our telephone directory, Mum reminds me. Four-petal primroses in the margins. Marginalia, they call it. Over and over again, like a ritual or penance. One, two, three, four and a stem; one, two, three, four and a stem. A wend of waves on paper. Telephones had curly cords back then. I'd wind and unwind ours around my index finger while Nan E. gabbed about her roses and those fucking aphids and why your grandfather is goddamn useless.

The letter X has the fewest listings in the phone book, along with Y and Z. The philosopher

René Descartes took advantage of their alphabetical position. Legend has it that in 1637, as he prepared to write his treatise on geometry, he used these letters to represent unknown quantities, while letters from the beginning (a, b, c) were used for known quantities. Fast forward 367 years to a Cornell University study, which finds that X is the fourth least used letter in English, occurring only 0.15 percent to 0.17 percent of the time. When I finish writing this book, I'll count all the X's. The real surprise is that J is the second least used.

X NOTE
Camp X, the unofficial name of a secret school for training covert agents during World War II, was also known as Project J.

J NOTE
There are 170 J's in this book.

Robert Capa, a founding member of the photojournalism agency Magnum, coined the term

Generation X. He used it as the title for a photo essay about men and women growing up immediately following World War II, published in 1953 and comprising twenty-four portraits. Capa explained, 'We named this unknown generation, The Generation X, and even in our first enthusiasm, we realized we had something far bigger than our talents and pockets could cope with.' In *GenXegesis: Essays on Alternative Youth (Sub)Culture*, John M. Ulrich writes that Capa's X 'is meant here to function primarily as a placeholder, a variable or blank to be filled in later.'

Poor X. Sometimes, she's little more than a proxy, a nothing occupying the position or place of a significant something. I do it as I type, inserting X's when I can't think of what word comes next, always three X's. Why I do this, I don't know. I can picture the idea of the word but not the word itself. X, then, is a word and a picture. She fills gaps, and a gap is also a kind of image. Nan E. starts banging on her coffin to catch my attention. Photographs can't fill gaps, dummy; they are lies in cuter costumes.

Except they can. A placeholder photograph *holds the place* until a better one, The One, appears. It's a dummy picture, a for-illustration-purposes-only picture, a may-not-be-an-exact-representation-of-real-life picture with too many 'toos' (too happy, posey, matchy-matchy). A picture masquerading as a yardstick of how life in a rectangle should look. How unrealistic is that? Pictures we toss from new photo frames and replace with ones of our our-ness. These our-pictures breed in larger rectangles we call homes, pictures our loved ones gush over and eventually stop noticing. Pictures that *hold our place in place.* Pictures that, after our death, pass to another, our our-ness becoming their our-ness.

Only one word starts with X and ends with *–ness*: X-ness, a term used by Plato to describe the form or essence of a thing in his Theory of Forms. Plato theorized that an X is an X because it imitates or participates in the Form of X (its f-ness). Bear with me; it's surprisingly simple to understand,

19

for which I have a former professor to thank. She described it as this: a rock is a rock because it imitates or participates in the Form of a rock (its 'rockness'). The Form of a rock is always a rock. Plato hypothesized that an X becomes more of an X—meaning it has more reality—the more fully it imitates the Form of X. Conversely, a thing has less reality the more it is removed from its Form. A better X has more f-ness or is closer to f-ness; a worse X has less f-ness. More reality equals more goodness. A grim logic follows: photographs have less goodness because they are things far from their Form.

Wow. Photographs have more in common with the letter X and my PFF—Philosopher Farmer Father—than I thought. PFF considers himself an ideas man. Colin the Farmer, can he fix it? Colin the Farmer, yes, he can! Wait. No, he can't. To be a farmer, you must have a farm. No farm, no farming. The farm-less farmer is formless. Where was Dad's big idea back then? There's no elixir for the formlessness I know he still feels, that Mum and I still feel—no photographs to fill those gaps. (Dad becomes a builder after leaving our farm.)

Can photographs fix anything? Mum asks. She suggests a nice cup of tea before I can answer. *Here a nice, there a nice, everywhere a nice-nice...* Dad mumbles about the hazards of bullshit philosophy and nice cups of tea.

In the 1980s, farm debt soared. Dad's loan contained a variable floating interest rate clause: *The Loan's interest rate shall float by X percent up or down without notice.* Your father's only option was variable floating, says Mum, flicking the threat of tears from her right eye. And sweetie, he can't swim.

Not Drowning, Waving was a rock band formed in 1983 whose lyrics focus on politics, seasons, and rural landscapes. 'Not made for radio charts and MTV rotations,' wrote one music correspondent, claiming that the band lived in musical *terra incognita*, an unknown or unexplored territory. They borrowed their name from Stevie Smith's poem "Not Waving but Drowning":

> Nobody heard him, the dead man,
> But still, he lay moaning:
> I was much further out than you thought
> And not waving but drowning.

Not Drowning, Waving recorded six albums, including the soundtrack for *Proof*, the 1991 film starring Hugo Weaving and Russell Crowe. It tells the story of a blind photographer, Martin, whose distrust of others stems from childhood and his first photograph: a man raking leaves in the garden. Martin's dying mother describes the view outside their window, telling him that it is Wednesday, the leaves are brown, yellow, and dark red, and a breeze is blowing the smaller leaves into spirals. Martin, unable to hear the scraping of the rake, is convinced his mother is lying. After she leaves the room, he takes a photograph as evidence that what he sensed differs from what his mother said she saw. He shows no one and hides it for decades as a reminder that people would exploit his blindness by lying to or pitying him. Near the film's end, Martin asks a friend, Andy, to interpret the photograph:

> ANDY: It's a man in a garden. It's a sunny day. The man is dressed in overalls and he's holding a rake. Beside him is a wheelbarrow. It's full of leaves. It must be autumn. There's something near the man's feet. A dog, I think. A bird bath. No birds in it, though. It's a small garden, neat. The man with the rake must look after it. I can't make out his face, but he looks old, and kind.

Like the famous Winter Garden photograph Roland Barthes describes in *Camera Lucida*, Martin's snapshot of the raking man is kept from us. This significant yet unremarkable object held

Martin in place, drowning him in suspicion and resentment. He lived a dead man's life.

My first photograph was of Brother BJ, a Gen Xer born in 1977. It's a color print, square, with rounded corners and a matte surface. He's seven years old, standing on a flecked grey stone path in Nan E.'s garden, wearing his favorite red polyester tracksuit with navy and white trim. His hands are folded in front of his slim body. He has fine, straight blonde hair and Air Force blue eyes. Behind him towers a mint bush with purple flowers (RGB 170, 114, 182). I kept this mesmerizing square sibling in a Little-Boy-Blue blue cardboard sleeve in the bottom drawer of my wardrobe, next to the heart-shaped double-sided compact mirror Nan E. gave me for my birthday. A square now retired to that enchanted, infuriating place we call *somewhere*. The mirror is long gone. Good riddance. It was the first object to prove I had huge pores like Dad and the first to remove a bit of self-love.

When the sun was too burn-blister white to ride our bikes around our farm, we played Scrabble at Mum's kitchen table. X and J are each worth eight points. I set down the letter tiles B-M-X. That's not a word. Yes, it is. No, it's not. Yes! No! Is! Not! LIAR! MAGGOT! Brother BJ flips the board and storms to his bedroom. I later learned that BMX stands for bicycle motocross. Bullshit, says Dad. It means nothing.

Everything means something. Mum whispers it after Dad leaves her kitchen. We play noughts and crosses to clear the air. I ask Mum why she always chooses O's. She closes her eyes, presses her left cheek into her shoulder, and, with her left hand, kneads the skin behind her right ear with her thumb. It's incredibly satisfying to watch and gives me that lovely, tingly sensation no one can explain. Because circles are love, she eventually says.

Noughts and crosses is known by many names: tic-tac-toe, XOXO, X's and O's, and Exy-Ozies. Some ascribe its origins to the ancient

Egyptians. Others link it to pagan rituals in the Middle Ages. The most tangible record of the game comes from the Romans. They called it *terni lapilli,* three pebbles at a time, which players moved around a grid. These grids can still be found scratched into surfaces around Rome.

Some of our family snapshots have X's and O's scrawled or stamped onto their backs. Mum can't remember now what they mean. They remind me of Old Jack Adams's beef cattle, their bodies seared with JA from his custom branding iron. In the Book of Ezekiel, God commands one of his prophets to inscribe the letter *taw,* similar in shape to an X, onto the foreheads of those citizens of Jerusalem who were his faithful servants. Those unmarked were slaughtered.

Do you think there's such a thing as a genuinely blank surface? I ask Mum. Even the emptiest surface has microscopic stuff in or on it. Perhaps our life's pictures form under our skin before birth, making little squeaks like eggs in boiling water.

I think we spend most of our lives sweeping memories from one surface to another, Mum says to the empty cups as she carries them to the sink.

Long before Olivia Newton-John's hit single, the word Xanadu appeared in the first stanza of the 1797 poem "Kubla Khan" by Samuel Taylor Coleridge:

> In Xanadu did Kubla Khan
> A stately pleasure-dome decree:
> Where Alph, the sacred river, ran
> Through caverns measureless to man
> Down to a sunless sea.

A sunless sea, what color she be? Lucifer Red or Antihero Green? No: a brume of blue that we can't see, not even in a 3,200-megapixel photograph made with imaging sensors inside the world's most powerful digital camera. A blue that probably lives in the Xanadu Hills of Victoria

Land, Antarctica, named in 1994 in connection with the adjacent Alph River, inspired by Coleridge's poem.

In 2015, at the opposite end of the earth, the photographer Louie Palu, also a Gen X-er, took photographs of snow blocks shaped into an X stained with red smoke grenades by Canadian soldiers and airmen. Brian Sholis writes in *Artforum*: 'Palu's evocative photographs provide needed insight into a place we can no longer afford to treat as a blank spot on the map.'

Isn't everywhere a blank spot on a map until photographed?

In the film *Citizen Kane*, Xanadu is the name of Charles Foster Kane's horse. It's also the name of an Australia-sized reflective region on the surface of Saturn's moon, Titan, first imaged in 1994 by the Hubble Space Telescope.

'Something blank' is the photograph *pre*-photograph, a dormant potential. I could be talking about myself as a blank spot in a sunless disquiet, not waving but drowning in history's shadow. I could be talking about Dad squatting in one of his lower paddocks, sieving potential from the soil, having signed his life to a loan that could only hold our bodies in place so long. I could be talking about earthworms who spend their life making more earth, unlike Dad, who buried himself in brownish debt and spoke a language of checkbook whites. Maybe that's what I hope to find in the chaos of boxes in his garage, a swell of bright and shiny all-knowing X-particles like those detected by physicists working at the world's largest particle accelerator near Geneva, Switzerland. Or a magic wand that, when waved, brings Fiat Lux, Latin for 'Let there be light.'

Let there be light: our earliest photographic wish.

The photograph is a way of seeing what we can't see from inside our bodies, writes Nicholas

Muellner in *Lacuna Park*. I'm not blind, but there are things I can't see (and don't know) when making photographs and things I can't see (and don't know) until something becomes a photograph. When I have an image of our farm in mind, I'm not far from the ideal. It becomes ideal through my imagining it glowing and full. Light lets love in. When it spews out of my camera as a photograph, it resembles a carbon sugar snake, but beautiful because it's my ideal.

Then blankness rolls in. Doubt exacerbates. My ideal clouds. It becomes the warp of trying on someone else's prescription glasses, the windshield of Dad's truck on a frigid morning. I try again. I hold open a big imaginary door for an image. *Come on in.* I put the viewfinder to my eye. I stand tall. The door shrinks, and the image watercolors into the welcome mat.

My camera, every camera, is a delusion machine. *I can help,* she promises. *Hold onto me, and you will hold onto time.* Instead, she produces a photograph, a paperweight of eyes and years. The ugly truth about any picture you make is that you won't always feel the same way about it. It can't hold you. It goes like this: *It's a good picture. It's great! I like That, but not That. It's good-ish. It has some merit. It's dumb. It stinks. It's too this/that/ the other thing. It's ridiculous. I don't like That. Or That. Still too much of That. Still not a keeper. I have to remake it. I have to go back.*

My camera is scarily good at wooing me. But, try as I may, I struggle to picture our farm, my Xanadu, through photographic stillness in a way that satisfies me. She defies the apparatus, forever a photograph not taken, the X-axis of the horizon where all the will-o'-the-wisps, trompe l'oeils, and pots of gold play. An idealized other of such magnificence and beauty, she rejects every overture I extend through my viewfinder. Viewfinder is a malicious little word.

Dad decides that Xanadu is a perfect name for a calf.

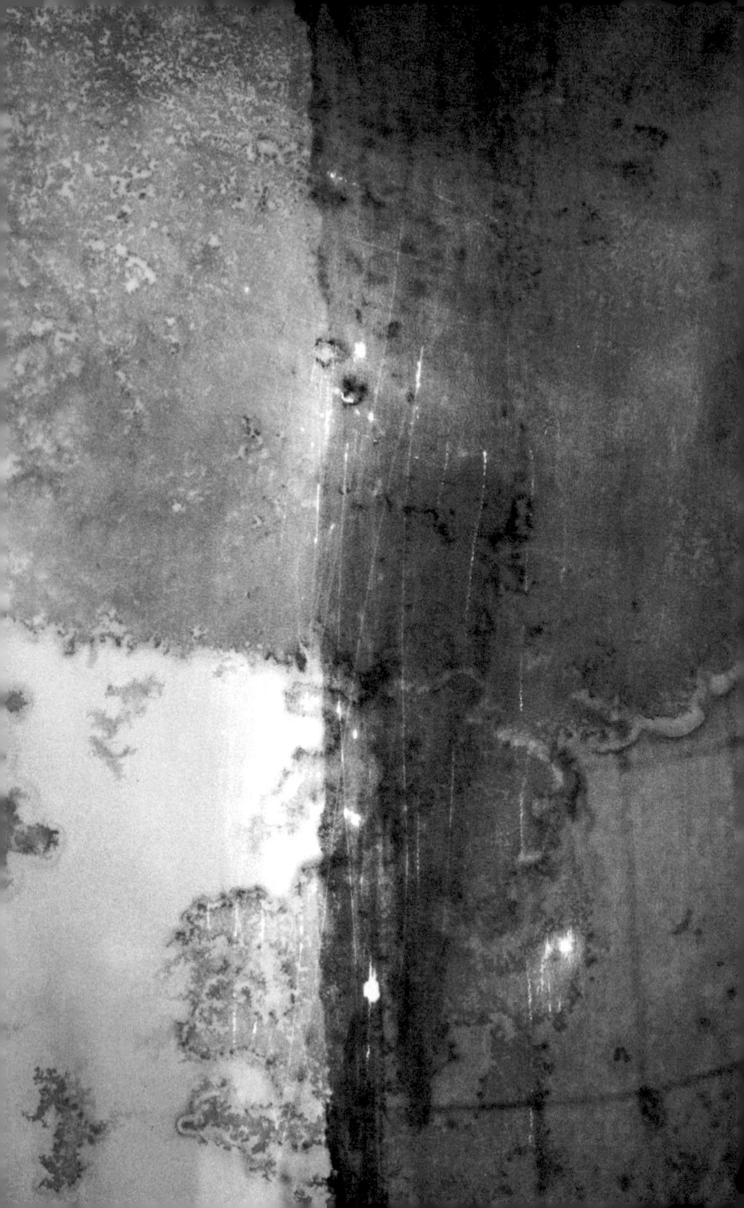

III

Cross your legs, say cheese!

Firsts are significant in amateur photography: firstborn, first birthday, first kiss, car, graduation. How we save and protect them through photography, memory, and speech ensures they last. In *Snapshot Versions of Life*, Richard Chalfen says, 'There are good reasons why family albums contain more pictures related to births than deaths, to achievements rather than defeats or disappointments. A family album shows all that is life-affirming and pleasurable while it systematically suppresses life's pains.' Chalfen never saw *our* albums—aftermaths, afterbirths, aftershocks, living happily never ever between vinyl hardcovers.

February 1979, your first day of kindergarten! Mum brings the album to her nose and squints. Oh, look, there's an X. She taps the surface of a photograph in which I'm riding my new 7X scooter. And here you are, barefoot, in your first school uniform.

PICTURE DAY, GRADE ONE

Male Photographer barks instructions—girls in front, boys behind. His female assistant forces a television-cohost-type smile. Like on *Wheel of Fortune!* Dad slaps Mum's kitchen table. What was her name, Thingamajig, that broad, the world's longest-running game show host? Mum makes a series of thinking noises through her teeth. Adriana Xenides! The table gets another slap.

PICTURE DAY, GRADE TWO

Girls, *GIRLS!* Male Photographer makes a closing V-gesture at us with his fingers. His female assistant scurries into the frame to show us how to slide our legs right over left.

Many types of leg-crosses mimic the letter X. The standing leg cross is usually adopted when you meet someone for the first time. The double cross is where you cross your arms and legs. With the figure four leg clamp, you lock one leg over the other and place both hands onto the raised part. I find other examples in Mum's albums: the ankle lock, leg twine, and parallel leg position. In almost every picture, the farmers have their arms crossed, which makes a flattened-out X shape. Some body language experts say this sends a negative message and that you're probably feeling stressed, insecure, afraid, or resistant by crossing your arms this way. Others say it's a form of self-hugging. Dad snorts. Or, we're just crossing our fucking arms.

PICTURE DAY, GRADE THREE

Mum enrolls Brother BJ and me at the new religious school. The photographic conditions of stillness and sameness remain—girls *still* sitting in the front row, the *same* leg-crosses, *still* a Male Photographer and his female assistant. Be still and know that I am God, Male Photographer quips. His female assistant rolls her eyes and hands out print order forms.

Print enlargements were not a thing way back when. Ambrotypes, cabinet pints, *cartes-de-visite*, glass plates, and minettes had fixed sizes, and frames and albums were designed accordingly. Everything was standard. I can still hear Male Photographer demanding we standardize. Straighten up, clean your glasses, stop frowning, sneezing, chewing, wriggling. What's with the bug eyes? Is that—dandruff? Can't you all just be the same?

Photographs can be double standards. The actor-director-turned-photographer Dennis Hopper's 1961 photograph *Double Standard*, taken through the windshield of a car at the intersection of Santa Monica Boulevard, Melrose Avenue, and North Doheny Drive, is a literal and symbolic duality. It depicts an eastward view at a West Hollywood intersection from inside the car, looking out at the junction of a fabulous future and a fuck-off past. A motion picture in a publicity still, signed and numbered in pencil on the back.

The exact origin of the X-mark as a signature is unknown. Some claim it dates back to the Middle Ages, that X means 'Christ,' so by signing X, you're saying, *In Christ's name, I assert*. The signee would kiss the X to prove that what was written in the document was genuine. Other document authentication methods included cutting a lock of hair or an act of violence, such as a slap across the face, to ensure those involved would recall the physical pain and associate it with the deal made. Signing an X was common practice with the illiterate. When the English poet William Blake married Catherine Boucher in 1782, the bride signed the marriage register with an X.

I remember practice-kissing the oversized poster of Michael J. Fox taped behind my bedroom door so much that his lips started to clump and disintegrate. No matter how sloppy I was, his expression never changed, his likeness asserting: *Odette, you are a good kisser.*

J NOTE
Michael's J is not a real J but an A for Andrew.

PICTURE DAY, GRADE FOUR

Dad trudges into Mum's kitchen, his over-alls covered in yellow streaks from spray-painting cows' legs with an X to identify those on penicillin so that he remembers to drain their milk into a bucket. He tosses his terry cloth hat across Mum's counter, looks at my school photograph, and grunts. You look cheesy.

One of the earliest written records of cheesing for a photograph appears in October 1943 in the *Big Spring Daily Herald*, a Texas newspaper. In the 19th century, the word you said in readiness for being photographed was 'prunes' to keep the mouth small and the face neutral and dignified. Back then, only children, peasants, and drunks smiled in photographs.

Auntie Mary pops by for a visit. She challenges me to a word duel. Words that rhyme with cheese, shortest to longest, go! Before I can think of a single word, Auntie Mary is in rapid-fire mode. Tease! Sleaze! Squeeze! Abductees! Guarantees! Idiosyncrasies! Now, words that rhyme with prunes, go, go, go! Moon! Immune! Macaroon! Opportune! Afternoon! Contrabassoon! I'm the winner! she declares with a shimmy of her shoulders. Auntie Mary excels at word games, and, being the sweet old dear she is, shows interest in my discovery of two kinds of cheese that start with X: xynotyro, and xynomyzithra, Greek whey cheeses made from sheep's or goat's milk and often served with prunes. Did you ever make cheese at the farm? Auntie Mary winks at me. She is a cheeky minx.

Not intentionally, says Dad, who looks at Mum, who gives me another trademark look I understand but have yet to photograph.

There is no cheesing in Brother BJ's school photograph that year. He sports a fluffy white patch over his right eye because he has strabismus, or crossed eyes. 'A child with strabismus rejects the image of the improperly aligned eye,' confirms Doctor Cowham, referring Brother BJ for his first pair of glasses. (Yes, a dairy farmer's children saw a doctor named Cowham.)

We reject images in many ways: deleting, turning the page, refusing to 'like.' We cut up snapshots of divorced parents and ex-lovers, sometimes taping them back together, making them look more loved, more real. Marilyn Monroe famously used an orange marker to cross out images she didn't want published in *Vogue* after her last sitting for the photographer Bert Stern. Taken at the Hotel Bel-Air weeks before her death, the photographs deemed unsuitable by Monroe have ironically become some of her best-known. Self-rejection via X's made Monroe even more desirable — the cancellation, in this case, sexier than confirmation.

PICTURE DAY, GRADE FIVE

Stand up straight and smile, say ch– SEX! The class clown interrupts Male Photographer with shutter-press precision. His female assistant swallows her giggles.

We farm kids thought we knew all about it. We saw bulls mount cows and dogs stuck together. We could identify the love songs of currawongs and the horny honks of geese and rabbits. Sex was auditory, rudimentary, and perfunctory. Farm walls were thin.

Sex education privileged the white heterosexual. We saw vulgar cartoons of male trains shunting female trains; that sort of bad taste. Boys snickered at the word cervix. There was no unisex, no mention of the letter X symbolizing the anus. In 2003, Alex MacFarlane became the first person to receive a passport listing the holder's sex as X for intersex, and it wasn't until October 2021 that the U.S. Department of State issued the first passport with an X gender marker.

PICTURE DAY, GRADE SIX

It coincides with bring-your-pet-to-school day—a huge mistake.

Veterinary surgeons frequented our farm. I eavesdropped on their conversations with Dad about X and Y chromosomes, X-rays, xanthosis (the turning of something yellow), the xiphoid process (the end part of the sternum), and xylazine, a drug for sedation. Today, Dad and Doctor David are talking about fetal non-standards called freemartins: a hermaphrodite or imperfect sterile female calf, usually the twin of a male calf. Farmer Chris over the hill has one, and everyone wants to see it. Doctor David keeps a Polaroid camera in his truck for such firsts. He shows Dad a photograph he took earlier in the day of Old Jack Adams's stud cow, Xara, who has a near-perfect X on her forehead.

I re-examine Dennis Hopper's *Double Standard* photograph. Walking my eyes right to left, I notice the speed limit sign. The tree in front of the Chinese restaurant. The grip on the steering wheel. Two Standard signs, chevron-shaped. The price of gas. A man waiting to cross the road. And the billboard between the traffic light and hospital sign, in which a mannequin-like white woman with an up-do, wearing a sleeveless black dress, holds a plated meal. The accompanying text reads:

Smart women
cook with Gas
In Balanced Power Homes

Because smart women *cook*. Smart women *dress up* to cook. Smart women say *prunes* for the camera. Smart women know Gas is Good. As for balanced power, the similarities between electrical loads and the farmer's view of femaleness abound. Power draw, consumption, overload, oh, the analogies. As with John Singer Sargent's 1884 painting *Madame* X — a bold image of an unabashed woman — Hopper's photograph featuring this so-called 'smart woman' is a study in opposition. Dad shrugs. It's all simple math: how to calculate ratios, miles per hour, men to women. What's the big deal? I will myself to breathe normally, but the memory of 1 Timothy 2:11 (which Dad had taped behind the bathroom door) shifts from back burner to front burner, simmer to boil: 'Let a wife learn in quietness in complete subjection.'

The lid of my pot blows blue-sky-high.

Our farming community has accepted standards of maleness and femaleness, especially in the division of labor. Males do male things, and females do female things *and* male things when required by males. Ambidextrous reproductive labor where females are the Jack and Jill of all trades.

Quiet Time. A handwritten caption on a series of snapshots from 1979 through 1985. Always Easter Sunday, Mother's Day, Father's Day, and Christmas Day. Always after lunch, after wash the dishes, dry the dishes, turn our feelings over. Just the XXs in our family: Nan E., Nana L., Mum, and me, seated in age order, wearing our best-behavior Sunday Best even if it was Tuesday. While the XYs napped in the lounge room, Mum set four chairs in front of her wood stove. We perched there like canaries who'd lost their songs, hands crossed in our laps. A singular form of silence, which photographs are, too, mute and prone to misinterpretation and symbolic violence. On these special days, we XXs wore our best feathery frocks, fitting and right, except for Nan E., who disliked dresses. She never crossed her legs and never, ever acknowledged the camera.

Genetic disorders occur from missing, extra, or malformed copies of the X chromosome. Thanks to a photograph called the karyotype, we can see them, but to get this picture, chromosomes must be isolated, stained, and examined under a microscope, then cut up and rearranged by size. What would a cytogeneticist make of our *Quiet Time* pictures? What would the English chemist Rosalind Franklin have thought about them? Franklin is best known for her work on the X-ray diffraction images of DNA, particularly Photo 51, taken by her student Raymond Gosling, which led to the discovery of the DNA double helix for which three men—Francis Crick, James Watson, and Maurice Wilkins—shared the Nobel Prize in Physiology of Medicine in 1962. After leaving King's College London, Franklin led pioneering work at Birkbeck University on the molecular structures of viruses. In 1958, the day before she was due to unveil new research at an international fair in Brussels, she died of ovarian cancer. She was 37. Franklin's team member Aaron Klug continued her research and (conveniently for him, as the rules were modified in 1974 to prohibit posthumous nominations) was the sole winner of the Nobel Prize in Chemistry in 1982.

Exasperated, I revisit notes from a workshop with the writer Eileen Myles, who told me to print a chapter, cut it up, and lay it out in order on a long table. 'This will help you consider what you like and identify any gaps. We don't need permission to be deviant in our writing,' Myles said. 'Make a list of all you could write about, no matter how unorthodox,' Myles said. *Write a song from a bird's perspective*, I'd jotted down. I remove the pencil from behind my right ear and gnaw on it. *Think like a bird, think like a bird.*

Set in early spring, a male cardinal sings to all the single ladies:

> Come fuck with me
> Let's fuck, let's fuck away
> If you can use some exotic juice
> There's a branch for our risqué
> Come fuck with me
> Let's fuck, let's fuck away.

I chew on *fuck* all afternoon until I can taste the lead. Then a glimmer: I learn that in the old

Russian alphabet, the letter X was called *kher*, from which 'fuck' came, meaning to cross something out on paper. Another theory is that *fuck* is of Germanic origin and related to Dutch and Swedish words for 'to strike' and 'to move back and forth.' The cherry on top is that *xep* (pronounced 'kher') in Russian means 'dick' in English.

PICTURE DAY, GRADE SEVEN (TAKE 1)

The camera flash exposes our white crossover training bras under our uniforms. A picture retake date is set.

PICTURE DAY, GRADE SEVEN (TAKE 2)

I'm plump and pimply with a frizzy crop and gold-tone crossbar glasses that make me look cross. Nan E. says I look like Dad, who says I look like the back end of the school bus. Mum orders one copy of the class photograph, and it's still a slap in the face whenever I look at it.

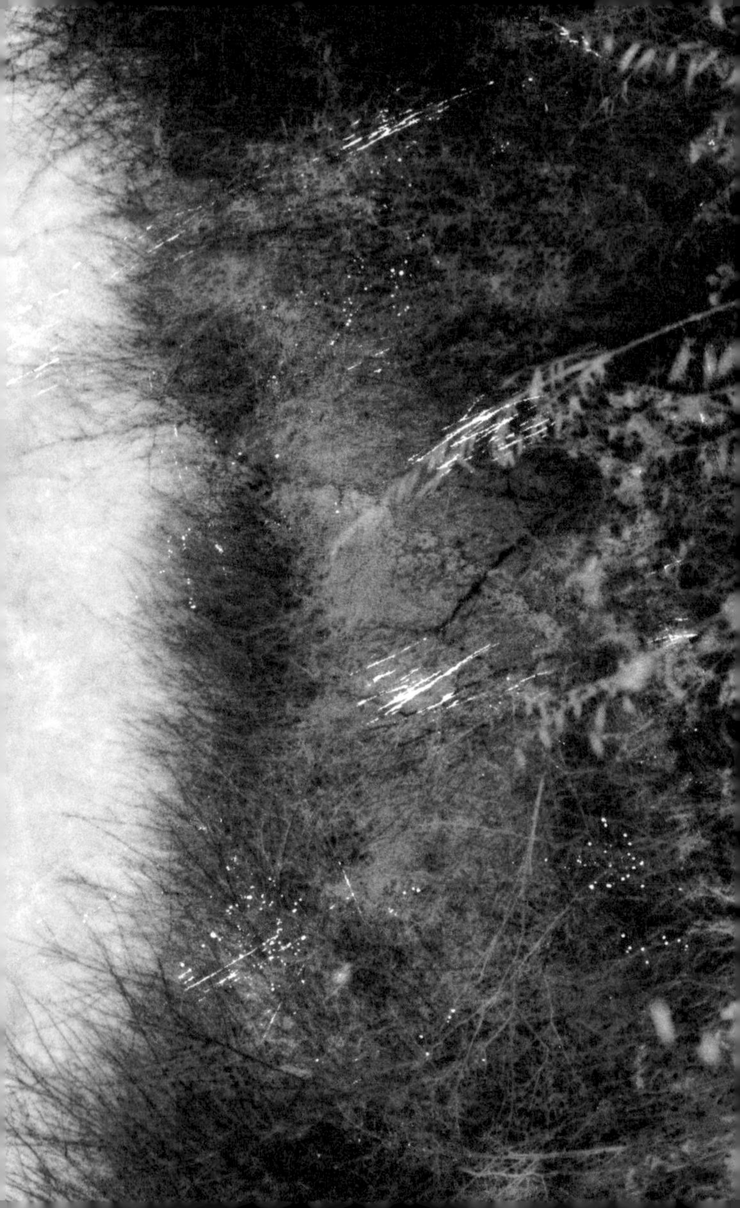

IV

Noxious

Dairy farmers worry. Seeds of unease sprout regardless of the season. They worry about weather, soil quality, and butterfat percentages. Drought, inflation, weeds. Incomings, outgoings. Mum worries they never admit to being worried.

Dad keeps his financial logbooks indexed in his brown filing cabinet in the northeast corner of Mum's kitchen. On top sits a jar stuffed with pens: black for profit, red for expenditure, and executive blue for denoting the difference. Black is good. We're in business! Red is urgent, act now, you're overextended, *wee-ooo, wee-ooo, wee-ooo*. There are no photographs of Dad scratching his chin, willing wads of cash to crash through the ceiling, feeling buggered blue.

Noxious weeds are pests. Agrichemicals are expensive. Dad's tin-clad spider-plagued Medium Shed chokes on *Ipomoea purpurea*, the common morning glory, and *Rumex hypogaeus*, the three-corner jack, an invasive fleshly plant that produces angry-looking seeds resembling a bull's head. Inside this shed are toxic concoctions that can quench or kill anything. Every bottle, can, and barrel is alphabetized and marked with a crude skull-and-crossbones sketch. Brother BJ and I recognize the universal symbol of death, but it doesn't stop us from double-daring each other to mix dodgy potions. Dad is cross but not surprised when we set his Medium Shed on fire.

The skull-and-crossbones design originated in the Late Middle Ages. It is *memento mori*, Latin for 'remember you must die.' The symbol extends to Christian catacombs and crypts, the lapels of the Secret Service, and Vanitas paintings.

In the German language, the word for skull-and-crossbones is *Totenkopf,* meaning 'death's head.' Initiation into Skull and Bones, the secret society founded in 1832 at Yale University, is rumored to take place inside a coffin.

Farm life is a life of daily death. When one of Dad's cows (My Girls, he calls them) breaks into the alfalfa paddock, she binges until her body resembles a hot-air balloon. Dad is selectively deaf around Mum but has no trouble hearing those ghastly, gassy groans. He wields his seax, aka the Scary Knife, to stab His Girl in the right spot to relieve the pressure. Too late. Dad chains her legs to the back of the tractor and drags her up to the Cow Drop. Later, he scrawls 'X2' on a piece of paper and sticks it to his filing cabinet with a magnet. It is a Termination of Lactation Code from an index printed on his monthly herd production report. D is for dry, as in dry due to disease. S is for sold: S2 for age, S4 for infertility, and S6 for poor temperament ('typical woman'). X is for

Died: X1 of disease, X2 bloat, X3 other, X4 notifiable disease.

Dad's younger brother Gary dies a few months later. On December 12, 1976, a drunk driver hits his Yamaha XS650 motorbike. Three days later, on doctors' advice, Nan E. and Grandpa turn off the life-support machine. Nan E. insists on arranging the funeral flowers. Peace lilies, carnations, and flax-colored everlasting daisies, also known as strawflowers, *Helichrysum bracteatum*, before being transferred to a new genus, *Xerochrysum*, in 1990. She writes a memorial notice for the local newspaper and clips and pastes it into a scrapbook. It becomes an annual ritual, writing, clipping, pasting, pressing strawflowers between pages, watching her Index of Grief grow. 'Find what you love and let it kill you,' is all she says when asked about the accident.

Uncle Gary's green helmet has an X-shaped mark on the top right of the visor. When Nan E. auctions the house after Grandpa dies, I beg Dad to buy the gruesome keepsake. The auctioneer's song continues long into the afternoon until every object is going, going, gone. The only souvenir Nan E. sets out on a shelf in her new flat is a miniature oval-shaped portrait of Gary. It now lives on Mum's piano, its melancholy blue background faded. Song-Sung-Blue blue now, says Mum.

Find what you love and let it kill you—a quote attributed to the poet Charles Bukowski and the musician Van Dyke Parks; also the title of an article by Mark Manson about the consequences of pursuing what you love. 'Doing what you love is not always loving what you do. It feels like an inevitability, like you have no choice because this is simply who you are, dysfunction and all. It's your chosen vehicle towards death.'

Right there, the camera: she is my vehicle. And yet, loving what I photograph and photographing what I love are incompatible.

Looking for bones? The Cow Drop is the place, a crater-like open-air coffin about thirty feet by thirty feet, a body of bodies. Every farmer has one in the highland where the sand is loose, granular and home to little else except *Opuntia* (prickly pear), *Solanum elaeagnifolium* (silverleaf nightshade), and *Salsola australis* (tumbleweed).

After the flesh decomposes, Dad teaches Brother BJ and me to identify and sort bones by shape, length, and weight. The coccyx, maxilla, proximal phalanges, even the thorax bones. I learn more about a cow's body than my own, buoyed by the many terms the farmer keeps in his Index of Slang for the women in his life: *cow, bitch, bat, vixen, duck.*

Auntie Mary's eyes flicker open. She has been snoozing at Mum's kitchen table. Isn't *index* one of the funniest words ever? Mum and I swap side glances. Auntie Mary giggles. In-dex, in-dex, in-*dex*! she sings while improvising a conga all the way to the loo.

Like the farmer's wife, the index lugs many definitions and responsibilities: list, guide, sign, gauge, scale, symbol, manifestation, token, measure, referent, number, arrangement, inventory, reference, integer, suffix, file, catalog, record, table, document, indicator, symptom, pointer, instrument, representation, adjustment, ratio, item. A town in Washington. An unincorporated community in Gilmer County, West Virginia.

The index: invaluable for locating and retrieving information, much like a photograph. Which is sometimes the only visual, material connection we have once a life dear to us ends.

As I write, I keep open a document I call the 'word grave' for all the scuffed snippets, almosts, and irrelevants I can't find a home for. Command-X for cut, -C for copy, -V for paste. It is my computer-based Cow Drop.

Before becoming a farmer's wife, Mum was a nurse aide trainee. Her hospital friends gifted her a mini medical encyclopedia. It lives in her kitchen, ready to answer niggling questions about bones, transplants, herpes, tropical diseases, and the Abortion Act. I check the index under X. There are eight entries, including the Xenopus Test, a pregnancy test carried out by injecting a urine specimen into *Xenopus laevis*, a female clawed frog that would lay eggs if the woman was pregnant.

Broken bones (and pregnancy) are inconveniences for the farmer, worse than weeds. Mum takes over when Dad breaks his left leg for reasons we can't discuss. Schooling must wait: I'm on full-time baking duty, cleaning, and digging up hundreds of *Oxalis pes-caprae* (soursobs) from the Kikuyu grass. Post-recovery, Dad is chasing me around his brown sofa. Mum is trying to watch the evening news. One of my toes catches a sofa leg and snaps. Dad blames Mum's heifer-ass. Mum sighs and fetches the frozen peas. Half an hour of cold compress later, she inspects the damage. The town is too far, the hour too late, and X-rays too expensive to confirm what she knows.

Wilhelm Conrad Röntgen put the X in X-ray. He discovered their potential for medical use upon seeing a picture of his wife Anna's left hand on a photographic plate on December 22, 1895, complete with wedding and engagement rings. It became the first photograph of a human body part using X-ray technology. When Anna saw the picture, she said, 'I have seen my death.'

I read this aloud to Mum. She looks out her kitchen window towards our farm, her woe-is-me blue eyes overlooking the cursive rain. The beautiful sparkle in my engagement ring, my heart and hand still grieve, she says, stroking her ringless ring finger. Dad pounces on the opportunity to fill the awkward silence. I've got an X-ray joke for you. What do dentists call their X-rays? Tooth pics!

Farm life is also a life of near-death experiences. By the age of eight, I'd almost drowned (twice), suffocated, endured burns and electric shocks, and eaten poisonous berries of the *Lycium ferocissimum* (African boxthorn). We discussed death like we did the weather, often in idioms: tits up, belly up, the wrong side of the grass. Counting worms. Gone bung. Bought the farm, Dad says.

Oh God. 'Bought the farm' is slang for 'died.'

Our pets were never 'sent to the farm.' We tossed them in the Cow Drop with a few *Arctotheca calendula* (Cape dandelions) for luck.

The death we knew had two gears: full-throttle frankness or blown-engine-dead, a no-longer-fixable, hard-to-find-parts kind of dead. But whoa, Nelly, *The End*? He was different. The End followed Mum closing the book's cover and turning off the light, a very different click from the camera shutter. It wasn't the end of the fairytale that bothered me (in our storybooks, demons ate your face off with a spoon). I was *terrified* of The Dark. Of all the gross, brutal, upsetting things that farm life exposes kids to, The Dark was my irrational Big Bad Foe. Bad-to-the-bone bad, scarier than Mr. X, scarier than The Scary Knife, scarier than any decaying animal. It explains why I was a frequent sleepwalker. Mum usually found me in her kitchen, opening drawers and cupboards. She'd ask what I was looking for, and I'd reply: Where's the light switch? Can you switch on the light? (*How to switch on a photograph?*) Then she'd lead me back to bed, put my bald once-primrose-yellow-now-old-duck-fat-colored teddy bear in my arms, and reassure me to sleep.

The photographer Sally Mann suffered Daddy-death nightmares. In her book *Hold Still*, chapter 24, titled "The X Above My Head," she describes a prophetic drawing she made in 1958, which she finds in a Kodak-yellow X-ray film box in her attic. It depicts her father sleeping on a sofa surrounded by a disparate cast of characters, including a rabbit and a circus pig. Everyone is smiling except a young girl with a letter X floating above her, beside which Mann wrote: *Wake up. Wake up, Daddy. Wake up, love.* I think about this story often, alongside what the photographer LaToya Ruby Frazier said during a lecture in 2020: *Take a black box into a dark space and look for light, for beauty.*

Two realizations cut across my wrists in the post-rain sun-flood from Mum's kitchen window: my fate, the fate of all photographers, is two black boxes—a camera and a coffin. And this doozy: the camera is a type of coffin, but rather than housing a dead body, it produces one.

Almost everything I drew, painted, collaged, and sculpted as a kid dripped with death and zealous expressions of sunshine. One of my first watercolors was *Rabbit in the Forest* (1979). A blackish-brownish blob with red guts soaking into the forest floor enveloped in end-of-life light. A glorious day to be dead. Out of all the art I made, Mum says she doesn't know why she kept that one, but I do. It's the rabbit-spew story, which she delights in retelling her friends, pastor, hairdresser, traveling salespeople, and strangers waiting in line at the store. I'm two years old, sitting on her kitchen floor, playing with a Tupperware Shape-O toy, and I decide it'd be fun to eat a cloth diaper pin with a decorative rabbit-shaped head. Mum sees me swallow it and sphinxes at her sink. Dad grabs my legs, hangs me upside down like a side of lamb, and shake-shake-shakes until the egg I ate for breakfast comes out, followed by what once was milk, then more eye-popping jolting until out drops the pin. He then sits me down in this sticky globular puddle and pats me on the head.

There are no photographs of that.

Unsurprisingly, my favorite X-ray photograph is *Neugeborenes Kaninchen (Newborn Rabbit)*, 1896, by Josef Maria Eder and Eduard Valenta, part of a portfolio they made less than a month after Röntgen published his discovery of

X-rays. 'In an era when photography's ability to accurately depict the visible world had become commonplace, this newfound capacity to record the invisible opened up a host of possibilities,' it says of the work on The Met's website.

Maybe that's why I was afraid of The Dark. I'd lie in bed, a vortex of worries twisting inside my boyish body, not about parental death or the invisible world, but that horrible chest-tightening feeling of being without the love of home. It's possible I knew then, before I really really knew, that the dark side of love would emerge only when I took my eyes and feet off our farm for good. Now, I return over and again, watching her die through my camera coffin, pruning small pieces of her body with the click of possession, overlaying memories of the good old days with today's antics of trying to make one decent photograph of her.

In *Ghost Image*, Hervé Guibert writes of an X-ray of the left side of his torso, taken when he was seventeen. It is more intimate than any nude, he says. He's right: intimacy and clothing have no intrinsic relationship. Brother BJ and I spent much of our childhood naked, chasing each other through the *Sorghum x Sudangrass* (Sudax) and lamenting the itchy red blotches (no photographs). I used to think having X-ray vision would be the best superpower ever until I realized that we are all porous whether clothed or not. Stuff seeps in and leaks out. Like the fictional curator with X-ray vision who Jonathan Lethem writes about in his essay 'X, Curator' in *History's Shadow*: 'X, Curator, had arrayed himself for the world and was naked nonetheless, like the artifacts he surveyed.'

Photographs are leaky, too, but obliviously so. They can't distinguish light from darkness, love from lust, intimacy from distance, clothed from stripped, or fantasy from reality. I could make some of these distinctions as a child, but The Dark made me feel anxious and exposed. As a radiographer, I could differentiate flesh from bone and maybe even detect death before death. Cool. Mum urged me down this career path. In time, I learned that being afraid of The Dark was its own superpower. I was conditioning myself to be better prepared for future losses, to make sure I lived to reproduce another day. *I was training myself to think like a camera.* I had to become a photographer and practice light, even if it meant working in a dark room.

I wish I'd known a photographer back then, not a farmer who took pictures but a photographer-photographer. The closest person to that was Mr. Speck, who safeguarded his Brand X weed killer with two padlocks fastened to his garden shed door. He lived to the east in an unpainted early-century cottage with an annex, which he'd converted into a museum of small animal skulls and glass bottles. Of the latter, Mr. Speck had hundreds of specimens, all indexed and accompanied by photographs in a leather journal he kept on top of his meat safe.

When Brother BJ and I excavated an old Vicks jar while digging behind Dad's chicken sheds, we walked it over to Mr. Speck, uncleaned

('Dirt gives us character,' he used to say). He was in his garden, hoe in hand, Voigtländer Vitomatic slung around his neck, marveling at his glads. Every year, he grew rows of hybrid gladioli. Mum remembers the name of just one, the *Gladiolus x colvillii*. Mr. Speck was grateful for our contribution and asked if I would pose for a photograph. I obliged; he produced shears from his back pocket, cut and arranged the flowers for me to hold, and pointed his camera into the halo of sunshine behind me. Brother BJ and I returned home with glads for Mum.

What happened to the sun-kissed photograph is a mystery. Mr. Speck died the following month—old age—and the State Trustee donated his glass bottles to the recycling depot in town. Today, Mr. Speck's shed is attacked by *Eragrostis curvula* (African lovegrass) and *Asparagus asparagoides* (bridal creeper). I have his Vitomatic. One of his nieces-who-isn't-really-a-niece passed it on. Mr. Speck had always intended his camera for me.

Dad's parents lived forty miles northwest of our farm. It was a magical journey reminiscent of the children's book *Bears in the Night*. Over the wooden ferry, across the plain of wheat fields next to the railway, up rocky outcrops dotted with *Opuntia* (wheel cactus), around big gum country. By 'magical' I mean after repeated vomiting into a dairy bucket wedged between my legs. 'It's all about parallax, just focus on the horizon or the trees in the distance,' was Dad's advice for dealing with carsickness. It's ironic. Motion parallax exacerbated my carsickness by making nearby objects seem to move faster, so I looked at faraway objects to ease it. Carsickness taught me about distance and perspective.

Dad still enjoys telling graphic stories about that railway line, cars wolfed by overland trains, and the fate of cows venturing too close to the tracks, evidenced by two pairs of femurs tied into X-shapes that hung below the signals for years. I think he timed our trips so he could stop, get out, and be lulled by the *buh-bum, buh-bum, buh-bum.* No photographs of that, either. The track was decommissioned in the 1990s, but I still stop and look both ways when I pass through, a journey tinged more with homesickness than carsickness.

Homesickness isn't a real thing! Dad snaps me out of my reverie. I check Mum's medical encyclopedia. Nothing. I get carried away searching other indexes. On the CDC website, under X: nothing. On the US Department of Health and Human Services website, there are only two X-entries: X-ray, and xylene poisoning. Homesickness, meanwhile, is an absentee. Homesickness is sick at home.

Kim Beil, a photo historian at Stanford, emails a picture of the entries listed under the letter X in Ziff Davis's 1939 *Glossary for Photography*. There are five: Xenar, X-ray film (*see* Film, X-ray), X-ray photography (*see* Radiography), X-rays, and Xylonite (*same as* Celluloid). *See, same as. Same as it ever was.* How funny. 'Same as it ever was' is a repeating line from "Once in a Lifetime" by Talking Heads. Brian Eno, who co-wrote the song, refers to it as 'the song with a funny balance, two centers of gravity.' Carsickness in a hit single.

Auntie Mary looks at me from over the top of her glasses. She's arranging *Moraea flaccida* (Cape tulips) into small vases. A stew of half-baked thoughts topples out of her mouth: Speaking of the letter X, does anyone play the xylophone anymore? I could use a cuppa. Damn, the bladder's giving me grief. Did you know that X-Files is rhyming slang for piles? Is there a cure for reflux? What's that hybrid tea rose called? Oh yes, the *Xaviere Tiberi*, evil little pricks everywhere. She performs an exaggerated head tilt toward Dad's sofa where the men sit. I tell Auntie Mary that there are more than fifty types of roses with names beginning with X, many of which are susceptible to mildew. She gasps and starts on gardening myths. Tea is a good fertilizer... caffeine kills the slugs... never move a peony plant... birdseed is a detox miracle... Who are you, Nurse Know-it-All? Uncle G. lobs from the sofa. The men break into big fat haw-haw-haws until Auntie Mary pitches a rich tea biscuit at Uncle G.'s head. Gotcha! She cheers and starts a Mexican-Wave-For-One.

Myths and old wives' tales are a lot like photographs. Supposed truths but spurious. They question realism against the possibility of magic, making concepts like death and homesickness easier, sometimes harder, to understand. And they're often stolen from women by men. Typical! Auntie Mary calls out. There is no response from the sofa.

Sometimes, X is the notice-me-fluorescent jacket or the half-block of cheddar front and center in Mum's fridge that Dad can't find. A 'something' meant to stand out, but we become accustomed to overlooking it, a 'something' at the mercy of scroll-to-top-see-same-as. I look at Mum, Auntie Mary, and the men, now cursing the television's black screen. It's the same as it ever was.

V

Here is how we met:

High school, 1988. That winter, during football practice, X. breaks his wrist so badly that the surgeon transplants pieces of his hip bone to repair the damage. When the nurses wheel him from Recovery to his room, X. is still groggy from the anesthetic. I stand at his bedside. He looks weak and small. Then, liking escalates to loving via a gesture so embedded in memory that if I close my eyes and refocus my current self, I am *there*. X. reaches up with his right hand and takes mine.

He doesn't open his eyes or say a word. We stay like that until visiting time ends. The ballooning of an iconic self-defining memory follows: a boy telephones me for the first time. We talk for ages, but the last five minutes outshine all else when X. asks: 'Will you be my girlfriend?'

X. arranges our first date. My clearest memories of that afternoon are object-related. The first is a gift, a teddy bear called Marty. The second is an event 'first': I photograph X. with Mum's Kodak Instamatic X-45.

Autobiographical memory and photographs share common ground. Both represent information about the past that can be experienced in the present. They act as triggers for other pictures and memories. When we hold the past in our hands as photographs, our present mentally looks back, and the *who-we-were* builds onto the *who-we-are* and *who-we-will-become*. Multiple futures erupt from looking, seeking, and imagining (and relooking, reseeking, reimagining). But self-deception lurks in every love story, especially first romantic love. We remember these in the most biased of ways. Every time we share the story, we add lashings of illusions and white lies like pizza toppings, so much so that the truth of any story about first love likely exists only when it's fresh.

The longer I study this color photograph of X. hugging the hood of this father's car, the more I realize I have shuffled and adapted my memories to fit with wishes and preferences I didn't know I had. In it, X. is shorter than I remember and rounder in the face. The car is parked under a golden elm tree (I don't recall any tree); it's not sunny (I am *sure* it was). X. is smiling close-lipped (I'd have put money on it being a toothy smile). The picture in my head differs from this square out-of-focus representation on textured luster paper. It is happier, sparkier. And it is fiction.

When I mentally time travel to Then, to us, I create a new 'us.' I restructure the self. A new/old world comes into view. Present and past blur as I reencounter my few snapshots of X. Memory, like the photograph, doesn't travel well without translation. Memory is the carsickness; translation is the bucket. Mental landscapes become victims of prejudice. We fetishize the content. We persuade, disguise, or self-justify as we do in using a camera. We are ongoing works of subjective and selective readjustment.

It is depression-blue blue but also a critical *aha* moment, how breaches and disparities in recollection—which the French philosopher Henri Bergson considers 'the diverse tones, rhythms, and intensities of mental life'—can be simultaneously troubling and touching. X.'s father's car is *in* the photograph, but I don't recall meeting him. I recall pressing the shutter, but details come from looking at the *image*, not remembering the event. I am looking deep into a photographic kaleidoscope of catch-22s.

Our first kiss happens at a birthday party sleepover. X. is wearing a striped rugby shirt, a detail I recall from a snapshot. I borrow Mum's Pentax and photograph my friends next to a shed covered in jasmine. Sunshine caresses their shoulders. The aroma of lilacs and sausages swirls around. Dragonflies helicopter. These details are only virtually available; the photograph is AWOL. After dinner and board games, our friends walk to a pine forest for menace-making. X. and I stay behind in the rumpus room. We are lying on a rattan sofa, listening to music. My head is on X's chest. I don't recall the song, or what prompts me to turn and look up, but when I do, he leans forward and kisses me. Even now, I can hear and feel those seconds. I am mentally picking petals from a primrose: *He loves me, he loves me, he loves me, he loves me, he loves me.*

Summer brings the first and only We-Photograph—a snapshot of X. and me, taken in December 1988. For years, I have played eye-spy inside this photograph, this annex to memory. *Something beginning with S: space.* A soft-focus room of delusion and nimbus. It marks unfinished business between the present 'I' and the past me. It speaks of us to me (perhaps photographs can talk?). Even as I hold myself in my hands, I'm not holding myself; I'm holding an image produced by the love that I was and still am in. I can wrap my arms (and love) around this photograph, and I'll fall through myself.

I am no match for this picture.

We look nothing alike. X. has short dark hair, plump lips, freckles, prominent gums, and pale skin. I have wiry brown hair I can't tame and white plastic-rimmed glasses too big for my face. X. wears aqua shorts and a vintage KISS T-shirt. Mine is a white T-shirt from Kmart. There's a cheap plastic watch around my left wrist. Our arms are positioned comfortably around each other; his on my waist, mine across his shoulders, though I look more relaxed than he does, and my smile is more smiley. This may owe to the person we're looking at: his younger brother, D. They tolerate each other but often fight, which may explain why X.'s eyes are narrower, and his lips barely curl upwards. We look at him; he looks at us. But I'm not *really* looking at D; I'm looking at my future and past. D. takes the photograph at my request. He's standing near the clothesline in their yard. It's mid-morning of a romance-blue blue day. There are trees in the background, but I can't remember (or identify from the picture) what type. We are centered. There's just the right amount of space above our heads. We are silent and still. We pose for posterity's sake.

Location played a vital role in our family snapshots. Most were taken outdoors, and 'firsts' were photographed near the homestead, often in front of Dad's fruit trees. This may explain why the We-Photograph was taken outside. I likely suggested the location based on traditions of image production. Informality and simplicity dictated our livelihood and, thus, our aesthetics. The photograph is pre-Internet and pre-cellphone. Film was expensive to process, so Mum urged me to be sparing. It was likely developed in January or February 1990. Upon becoming a print, the We-Photograph lived in the top drawer of my dresser. Today, I notice a handwritten caption, partially scribbled out. *Dear X.* and six little X's as kisses are all I can distinguish. This photograph was meant for X., a gift never given.

Dear Miss Emily
James Galvin, 1951

I knew the end would be gone before I got there.
After all, all rainbows lie for a living.
And as you have insisted repeatedly,
The difference between death and the Eternal
Present is about as far as one
Eyelash from the next, not wished upon.
Rainbows are not forms or stories, are they?
They are not doors ajar so much as far—
Flung situations without true beginnings
Or any ends—why bother—unless, as you
Suggest—repeatedly—there's nothing wrong

With this life, and we should all stop whining.
So I shift my focus now on how to end
A letter. In XOXOXO,

For example, Miss, which are the hugs
And which the kisses? Does anybody know?
I could argue either way: the O's
Are circles of embrace, the X is someone
Else's star burning inside your mouth;
Unless the O is a mouth that cannot speak,
Because, you know, it's busy.
X is the crucifixion all embraces
Are, here at the nowhere of the rainbow's end,
Where even light has failed its situation,
Slant the only life it ever had,
Where even the most gallant sunset can't
Hold back for more than a nonce the rain-laden
Eastern sky of night. It's clear. It's clear.
X's are both hugs and kisses, O's
Where stars that died gave out, gave up, gave in—
Where no one meant the promises they made.
Oh, and one more thing. I send my love
However long and far it takes—through light,
Through time, through all the faithlessness of men,

James Augustin Galvin,
    X,
His mark.

This is the photographer Dan Estabrook's favorite poem. I think about rainbows and their similarities to photographs. All photographs *lie for a living.* All are *flung situations without true beginnings or any ends.* All *slant life.* I like this a lot. Of course, I relate it to the slanting strokes of the letter X. *All,* a word that suggests inclusivity. But photography is not inclusive, nor are rainbows. Theoretically, every rainbow is a circle, but only its upper half can be seen from the ground. In theory, every photograph is complete, grounding, and whole.

In theory? What a bullshit phrase, curses Dad.

Fingers crossed! Mum calls out from her kitchen. At last, Dad has agreed—*in theory*—to let me help clean out a small section of his garage. I spend the afternoon sifting through layers of paper ruins until I find X.'s sole handwritten letter to me, still folded into fourths, written over two pages torn from a spiral notebook. This letter knows our love through my too-muchness. The emotional and physiological excess of unfolding and refolding, discoloration and fragility, halftones, and gentle creases everywhere, like those around my eyes. I absorb every detail with every bit of my body. This letter is my Victorian avatar.

Dear Odette. I taste every syllable. X. is a good writer. He's straightforward and factual, yet his voice is warm and vulnerable. He starts with a sympathetic opening. Avoids adjectives. No fluff or gush. With each new idea, he creates a new paragraph. Includes a story or two, a compliment or two. I bring the letter to my face and inhale. There is the faintest scent of his mother's laundry detergent. Then I press it to my chest where it hellos my heart. It is more precious than the We-Photograph by miles, years, or whatever measure of space and time a handwritten love letter occupies.

Mum instructs me in letter-writing etiquette with her keep-in-touch blue typewriter, a

Remington, reserved for special occasions. She explains that after signing off, add xoxo or five X's if they are someone very dear to you. More than five X's is too many. Always use lowercase, and don't forget to write SWALK across the envelope flap before mailing, but only when writing to your true love.

X and O, our binary love code. The Oxford English Dictionary attributes the first recorded use of X as a kiss to the British naturalist Gilbert White in a 1763 letter which ended, 'I am with many an xxxxxx and many a Pater noster and Ave Maria, Gil White.' Some disagree with this claim, stating that the X's refer to blessings rather than kisses. More than a century later, the letter X as a kiss becomes clearer. In an 1894 letter by Winston Churchill to his mother, he writes: 'Please excuse bad writing as I am in an awful hurry. (Many kisses.) xxx WSC.' One of the earliest confirmed mentions of an O for hugs is in a 1905 Missouri Supreme Court case—The State v. James E. Kelley.

The evidence includes this letter:

> 10,000 million X O
> Yours forever
> I will kiss Cicil for you now.

And in the court record: 'Prosecutrix, her mother and a banker in Bolivar testified that this letter was in defendant's handwriting. Prosecutrix also testified that the defendant told her that when he wrote X and O, he meant hugs and kisses.'

Mum writes X's and O's across the pad she uses for her weekly shopping list. She pauses to assess each line. I let my eyes fall out of focus. When you duplicate a letter X, what does it become? A chain-link pattern, a fence of barb, a hypertext city, a row of paper doll cutouts holding hands, nameless, faceless, silent like a photograph. O's without X's looks odd, Mum declares. You can have kisses alone, but hugs? Dad rolls his eyes. Just sign your damn name; everything after that is irrelevant. But what if you have an afterthought? Mum asks. That's why we have a P.S., I say. You mean B.S., says Dad. Mum autopilots her way to the kettle.

Dad always has to have the last word, even if it's a groan, cough, or fart on his way out the door.

Everybody knows that the dice are loaded. Everybody rolls with their fingers crossed. These are the first two lines of "Everybody Knows," a song by Leonard Cohen. 'Fingers crossed' is more than a common expression; it's a superstition. Witches cross their fingers to focus their energy and convey their possession of special powers. Crossing your fingers to wish for luck can also mean that if made behind your back, you just told a lie. I have caught my daughter crossing her fingers to invalidate a promise (I'll clean my room today) and as a pretext for fibbing (I already brushed my teeth). When I challenge her, I'm met with the plea: There's a difference between mistakes and lies, Mum! Oh, she's good.

Some consider the first or last line of a song, novel, poem, or movie a sign of greatness. A person's final social media post before their death has come to occupy a similar space, an example being the American rapper XXXTentacion's Instagram post in June 2018, a self-portrait captioned LOVE IS WAR and the twelfth most-liked Instagram post ever, with over 34 million likes. Gives you the willies, right? The idea of writing something profound, without knowing it's profound *because* you're about to die...and then actually *dying*. The writer in me (she is not me, *in theory*) rues last words. I can't think of an inspired anything on which to rest in peace. In pieces, maybe.

'"Between the useless words," she promises, "you'll see what I saw."' It's not the first or last line of John Berger's novel *From A to X: A Story in Letters*, in which the main character, Aida, writes to her imprisoned lover, Xavier. But it quite beautifully stresses A'ida's annoyance at the limitations and inadequacy of language and her desire to find the right words to tell Xavier all she sees and feels. It reminds me that words and photographs are hoodwinkers, all too good at reiterating estrangements. Looking at the We-Photograph reminds me: X. is your ex, and you are his ex, and that's the way it should be. It's useless to describe or covet it, and here's the kicker: At some point, all photographs become useless. Not useless as in inadequate, pathetic, or needing a second chance (oh, how I longed for that). Useless, as in unnecessary.

Mum had one of those microcassette recorders, like Columbo used, for dictating notes while driving to and from our farm after taking a job in town to help pay the bills. When X. came to stay during the school holidays, we recorded useless messages to each other, laughing at how tinny our voices sounded on playback. Most of our banter is lost to the plow of memory and overusing the rewind button, but I recall X. whispering I love you, and those being the last words on the tape. Somewhere, in another of Dad's boxes, at another time, I'll find that cassette.

I've unwritten and rewritten this chapter, omitting juicy tidbits to protect X.'s identity. Writing about someone you love in police-report terms is deadening. I prefer to write about stealing cigarettes, the dangers (and pleasures) of vegetable peelers, the bliss of back seats. To describe every supple, tender detail. But it is too much muchness. Also, there is the simple will to keep much of the us-ness and what happened to our us-ness to myself. And so, I stick to the surface, for that's how I know X. now. He's awake and available when I dream about him—which I often do because that's where I'm allowed to love him. He is freckly, gummy, and lovely, playing "I Was Made for Loving You" on his saxophone. He is throwing his tennis racquet at his brother. He is trying on a tuxedo for the first time. But over time, he is also fuzzier, more like a photocopy of a photocopy: a materialized aspiration, a poor carrier of what is real. Mental Xeroxing is the gauze bandage on his healed left arm. It is the 50-denier tights I wore to school in that winter of 1988.

I'll dream about him until I die, always seeing him as Then and only Then. My imagination refuses to push past that land of make-believe. Each time I look at the We-Photograph, memory stalemates. X. is the greater-than in our equation. The feeling is akin to realizing what's happening in the films *The Sixth Sense* and *A Beautiful Mind*. The *ohhhhh* feels good and then bad.

On paper, X. froze time in 1988.

Tonight, I could smell his mother's laundry detergent in my bathroom. It was a brief euphoric hit of time and place. I sniffed around the room for the source. I left and returned over and again, inhaling and smiling. Scents are challenging to put into words; we're not taught to read them the same way we are photographs. In the film *Jack & Sarah*, Amy asks Jack what he will tell his infant daughter Sarah about her namesake mother, who dies during childbirth. 'Everything, I suppose,' he says. 'I've kept her hairspray for Sarah to smell when she's older because that's how I remember her... It's silly....' Amy replies, 'No, you can't smell a photograph.'

I am that person who wonders what would happen if X. showed up at my door and asked me to come back to him. One version of me, the vertical upright me, shakes my head and stays put. Another version transforms into a photograph and feathers to the ground. X. picks me up, slips me into his breast pocket, and takes me home to his top drawer. I live forever underneath his favorite socks. X. smiles at me daily as he gets dressed, a bittersweet touch of his eyes befalling my flushness. I become his title case One, the selected and isolated One, the photograph as a lover. Living in his drawer, I see how I look with my eyes closed. I spend the rest of my day mentally undressing him.

As for the last line of X.'s handwritten letter, his mark? You already know.

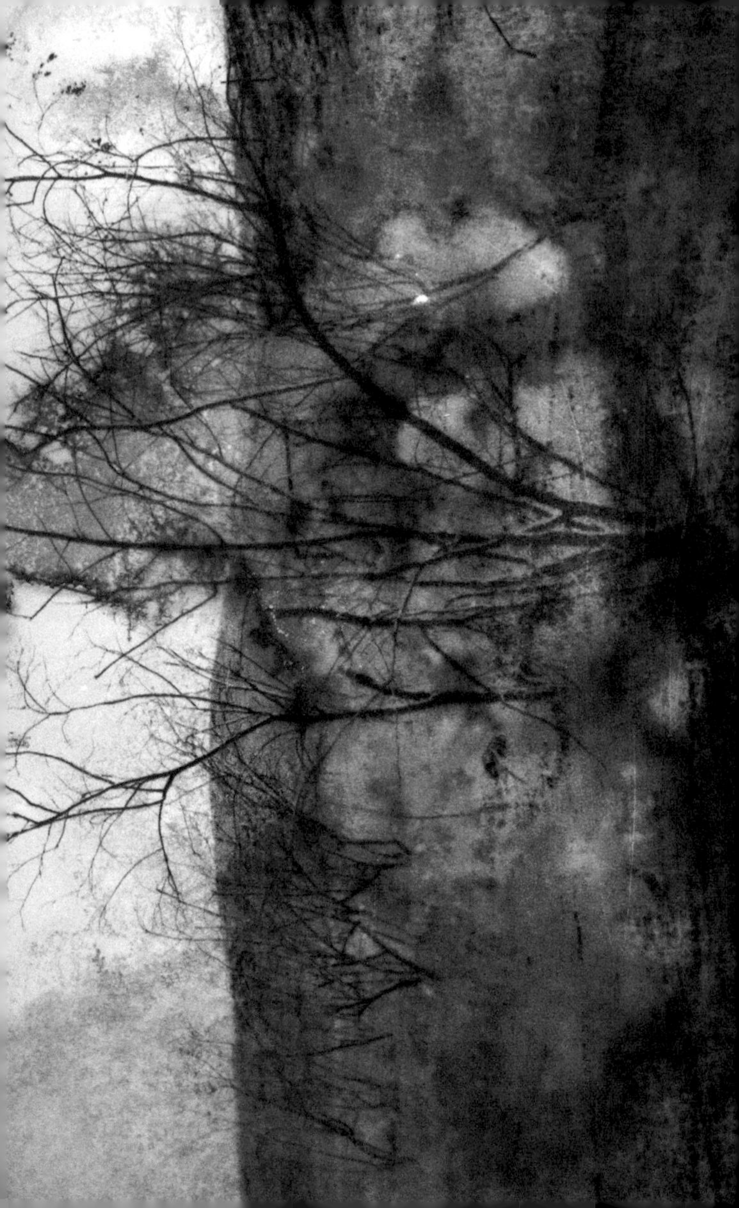

VI

Good and bad things come in threes

The Courtney Stephens short film *Ida Western Exile* begins with Georgia O'Keeffe discussing her love of northern New Mexico: 'It's something in the air; the sky is different, the stars are different, the wind is different. I shouldn't say much about this because other people may get interested, and I don't want them interested.'

O'Keeffe's painting *Blue Lines X* has a palpable something different, perhaps owing to her search for what the philosopher Thomas Leddy calls a quality of rightness, the X factor, the thing we can't describe that makes it *It*. In O'Keeffe's words: 'It was first done with charcoal, then there were probably five or six paintings of it with black watercolor before I got to this painting with blue watercolor that seemed right.'

There's a place near our farm where my something different lives. Set in undulant hills behind a small town—not even a town, a truck stop between other small non-towns—winds a farmers' shortcut. On this unnamed out-the-back track is My Olive. I've photographed My Olive for almost a decade, from different angles at different times of the day with my phone, my old Hasselblad, new Hasselblad, old Mamiya, and new Mamiya, all from the same spot where Mum uses her Lumix to take reference pictures of me taking pictures.

I noticed the tree immediately, telling Mum what the photographer Marion Post Wolcott told her husband, Lee, many times: 'Pull over, pull over, I see something!' My photo-eyes switched to a high beam. I saw My Olive. There are over two hundred and seventy synonyms for 'look' in English, but none describes my first look at her with the right quality of rightness. My Olive, a slow-growing body, safe from chainsaws, eager pests, and the itch-relief rubbings of cows. The west winds of spring reveal her silvery highlights (and my own). When it rains, the water pools and tickles her ankles. It is the perfect place for her. It's hard to believe life could be so simple, yet it is — a life of the pensive, meditative, and deep. I started calling her 'My Olive' after a friend commented, 'I love this long-term portrait study.'

When I look at My Olive as a *photograph*, I don't 'see' her at all. I see me. I see my parents (more Mum, for Dad doesn't love My Olive as we do). I see my daughter's likeness, long limbs and little hairs springing in all the right places. I see the grain of every visit to her surface, casual glances to intense gazes stacked into the mind's untidy archive. Of all the portraits taken of My Olive, I can't beat the first one made on Kodak T-Max film. Like the We-Photograph of X., this first prevails. 'First' has a privileged status. 'First' is blue-ribbon blue. Just ask the letter X, the third-to-last letter of the alphabet (for which there is a useless word: *antepenultimate*).

I'm not the only artist with an olive fetish. In April 1889, in Arles, France, before moving to the asylum in Saint-Rémy, Vincent Van Gogh wrote one of many letters to his brother. 'Ah, my dear Theo, if you could see the olive trees at this time of year... The old-silver and silver foliage greening up against the blue. And the orange-ish plowed soil. It's something very different from what one thinks of it in the north—it's a thing of such delicacy—so refined. It's like the lopped willows of our Dutch meadows or the oak bushes of our dunes, that's to say the murmur of an olive grove has something very intimate, immensely old about it. It's too beautiful for me to dare paint it or be able to form an idea of it.' Van Gogh studies the olive trees, takes his eyes and ideas for walks around the grove, and eventually finds the courage to complete fifteen paintings. The Van Gogh studio in Amsterdam notes, 'Van Gogh's olive trees are not as famous as his sunflowers, but they have become *his* olive trees.'

JoAnn Verburg has taken photographs of olives in Italy since the mid-1990s. In the Princeton

Art Museum collection, her diptych *X (Olive Trees)* comprises two chromogenic prints that reveal a subtle X when put side by side.

There's no official term for a fetish of photographs or photography (or olives), but there are fetishes related to difference. Xenophobia is a dislike of, prejudice against, or fear of strangers or people from other countries; its opposite, xenophilia, is an extreme attachment to foreign things.

'The past is a foreign country: they do things differently there.' This is the first line to L.P. Hartley's novel *The Go-Between*, which speaks to youth, love, and the dangers of secrets and memory suppression. Whenever I've lived far from home, my parents have acted as intermediaries for our farm and me. They go, look, walk, take pictures. Mum is happy to stay and report back. Dad is always eager to leave. I beg them to keep returning for many reasons, but one that hits home is my worry that our farm will one day become foreign to us — foreign as in *external*, like a foreign body that my curiosity as a child led me to shove peanuts up my nose. Our eyes will no longer be farm-fresh-egg-fresh, and I won't ever be capable of performing the right kind of photographic rightness, whatever that 'right' is.

Photographs can't know their birth or birthright. I wonder about the right of possession or privilege a photograph has from its delivery out of the camera. I also wonder about the camera as a parent or life-giver, only to birth a stillborn. I remember the awe I felt when the photographer Adama Delphine Fawundu talked about how our bodies are co-opted by ancestry and history, how others place things onto our bodies, and how we use our bodies to correct, covet, and complicate the past, especially our own.

A *ding* from my inbox. *It was 4 pm, and tea was cooked, so we visited Your Olive, sweetie. The light was perfect, or at least we thought it was. See what you think. It's grown since you were here. I also took a short movie because three lambs were bleating in the background. On the other side of the road was a giant kangaroo. I took many photos of Your Olive, so I will only send a few unless you want them all.*

Yes, oh yes, I want, I want them all so badly. I watch and re-watch thirty-six seconds of My Olive waving in the wind. Mum pans left, right, left. I wave back; my heart plays B minor on a cello. I turn off the light and cry myself to sleeplessness.

Nana L. says having two olives in a martini is bad luck. You must have three. Not that Nana L. is a martini drinker or drinks alcohol, period, but this two-olive thing she knows from her vast knowledge of bad luck, which she says all good grandmothers know. Cutting down sunflowers, crossed knives on the table, shoes on the table, peacock feathers, garnets, dried flowers—especially daisies—foxgloves, leaning ladders, black cats, broken clocks, green paint, taking photographs at funerals, rocking chairs, red pills, unmade beds, and on it goes. She says death and the letter X are the ultimate signs of bad luck. Do you have an X on your palm below your middle finger? Nana L. once asked me. I showed her my left palm. She fetched a fresh bar of borax soap and started scrubbing. Don't forget magpies; they're terrible bad luck. She pauses and gives her waggy finger a workout. They're the only birds that didn't sing when Jesus was crucified.

Mum's parents live in social housing near the highway. They also live on too many pills for too many conditions, including a pill for taking too many pills. One day after school, while Nana L. folded sheets, Brother BJ and I redecorated her kitchen with every bad-luck item we could find. It's the only time I saw Nana L. spasm with anger. She couldn't sleep that night until her neighbor Maria performed a healing ceremony to break the jinx.

X can be good and bad at once. A strike in baseball is bad for the batter; a strikeout is worse.

In ten-pin bowling, a strike is good. Three of our family pins fall within three years. Nana L. dies first (heart failure), then Pop (complications from diabetes), then Nan E. (dehydration, but officially suicide). Mum hires Old TV (Ted, the Videographer), for the first two funerals, which he records on VHS tape in HD-X. Mum ends up recording audio on her phone for Nan E.'s funeral because Old TV dies in the meantime, and no one else is willing to do it because they consider it bad luck.

HD-X, High-Definition Extra, means better quality. I know: who needs more detail, better color processing, less pixelation, and better encoding for a family funeral? And let's go there: what makes a funeral 'better'? Velvet cushions on the pews? A live choir? Overpriced organic olives on sustainably sourced bamboo cocktail picks? Footage of white handkerchiefs limp in hands before cutting to a baby content in its weeping mother's arms? Strangers clutching each other as a uniformed trumpeter plays "The Last Post"?

How does a photograph hold another photograph? Who is the photograph's significant other?

A funeral is an exhibition of rectangles: coffin, hearse, church, furnace, grave, shovel— and photography. There's a lot there-but-not-there in this picture I hold, taken at Nan E.'s funeral. It's April, the sky is apparition-blue blue. Jonquils and crocuses pray together. A canopy offers protection from the risk of showers. There are blue-black suits, pants, shoes, and clusters of hair in whirlpool, coin, and ice cap colors, including Pastor Andy's jaw-skimming beard. Uncle J. reads a short obituary with some light-hearted parts at the end, and, says Mum, he breaks only at 'and we will miss her.'

Edgar Degas said we were created to look at one another. Except at funerals, it seems. In this photograph, nobody looks at Nan E.'s casket, surrounded by a hyper-green faux grass cover held in place with four X-shaped weights. Almost everyone looks at the ground, hands in pockets or folded in front of their privates, their bodies forming a puddle-shaped frame. It's as if we can't bear to acknowledge the vertical living in the face of the horizontal dead. There is stiffness in every posture. When someone dies, parts of us fossilize and become rooted to the earth like the statues we shoulder in the cemetery. We see where our bones will one day soften. *We turn into living photographs.*

The actor Tilda Swinton keeps me company via YouTube, talking about backdrops and frames and why this cushion—she picks up the one next to her—is 'here' and not 'there.' She says the position of one's body inside a frame is less interesting than what we mentally add to the scene (true), that we can only transform ourselves when we forget about the ground, and that we always carry context with us, or should.

The context isn't goodbye in this photograph of Nan E.'s funeral. It is hope for the living, the realities of reframing death, the objectification of a body in four-sided silence. I pause Tilda and

relisten to the audio recording. I hear magpies war-
bling in the pines planted on the cemetery's eastern
boundary and seize the memory of their unmis-
takable scent. It catapults me back to forest walks
with Grandpa. He'd stretch out of his yolk-yellow
Toyota, adjust his boots, and recite Psalm 23:4.
*Yea, though I walk through the valley of the shadow
of death, I will fear no evil, for you are with me.*

How often does the letter X appear in the
Bible? Mum places cups of tea before Dad, Auntie
Mary, and me. In the King James version, X
appears 1,436 times but never at the start of a word
(in the Book of Esther, the Persian King Xerxes I is
referred to as King Ahasuerus).

At least you got back that first photograph of
BJ after Rella killed herself, Dad says. He always
sees the sunny side-up of death, or claims to. Mum
cocks her head, slow-blinks like a cat, and changes
the subject. It's true; the first photograph of baby

Brother BJ, taken four weeks after an emergency Caesarean section and kept (stolen) by Nan E., had found its way home. It was our family's longest-running photo bone of contention, usually ignited during the holidays, Nan. E. arguing with Mum over the right way to roast chicken, save money, and discipline us kids (that topic was a crowd-pleaser). This hot-potato photograph now lives in a cold archive box marked 'Rella's Xtras' in the under-stair cupboard in Mum's kitchen.

It's weird. Sometimes, we want something so badly—in this case, a creased, overexposed black-and-white photograph of a young woman holding her undersized, still-runny-in-the-whites baby—that when we finally get it, its importance has run out of steam. Our mind has wasted years mushrooming a version of the real thing so juicy and delicious, so *right*, that we've doomed it to fail. That photograph of baby Brother BJ, once prized, is now little more than memory fungus.

Later, I snoop around that cold archive box of Xtras and find three small photo albums labeled *Photos for Paintings* in Nan. E's ribbon-like handwriting. They are filled with images of trees: red gums, blue gums, eucalypts, wattles, and figs. Living trees, tree corpses, trees in pots, phallic trees. A digest of dendrophilia, much like John A. LaMacchia's *X-mas Trees*, a photobook on the life cycle of the holiday tree that ends with tree body bags dumped at the curb.

Did you know trees make a crying-type noise when starved of water? Uncle J., a botanist, asks me via FaceTime. It's an ultrasonic sound too high for the human ear to detect, so it goes unheard. Trees rely on bundles of special tubes called xylem to drink, which lift water and dissolved minerals from the roots to the highest leaves and branches. Because many trees grow tall, liquid in the xylem can be under intense pressure. I tell Uncle J. about Peter Hutchinson, a British-born artist who lived and worked in Provincetown, Massachusetts. His 1974 photobook *Alphabet Series* features each letter alongside a corresponding photograph. For X, it's xylem necrosis, the death of this life-giving tree tissue. Uncle J. then gifts me a new X-word—xylography—the art of making engravings on wood blocks for printing.

Two color photographs in Nan E.'s *Photos for Paintings* perplexed me for weeks. They depict the same rural scene seconds apart. Shot on Agfa film, frames two and three, according to text on the back. Each shows a conglomerate of boulders dotted with lichen, in front of which runs a fence made of three rows of cyclone wire topped with a track of barb. Splintered pine columns, steel droppers, and rectangular concrete pillars support the fence. Dry grasses in varying shades of rust hide the soil. A gravel road curves right. Pewter clouds suggest an impending storm. Behind the boulder with a long crack is a dead tree, warped and left-leaning. Adjacent is a shorter, thicker-trunked tree. The photographs are taken from the passenger side of a car. I examine them for so long that they become Magic Eye puzzles. I know these rocks, these trees, but from where, when? The kinks and knots of memory refuse to cooperate. I know the photographs know this. I have to forget before I remember.

Seven months later, memory irons out. These photographs were taken along a back road near My Olive. Our trees are friends. They are pen pals on the wind's breath.

Dad had a taxonomy and a particular can of write-off-white paint for marking dead trees. X for a lightning strike, F for fire, I for insect infestation, A for age, P for poisoned, and K for fuck knows. A zig-zag pattern meant time to grab the axe. He tasked Brother BJ and me with cross-stacking logs and assembling sticks into the ideal X-shape for winter fires. You need the right amount of space to get the air up there, like a tart's short skirt, heh, heh, heh.

My Olive grows in a wildfire zone. I worry she will perish at the licks of famished flames. We are taught at school that trying to outrun a fire is bad luck. A wall of flames can move at up to twenty miles per hour. I hold this thought while holding a color photograph tucked behind another in one of Nan E.'s albums. It's of a young man wearing a candy-striped bucket hat running from a raging grass fire. I pass it to Mum, who removes her glasses. That's Uncle Gary, says Mum, and I took it with my Instamatic. She nods as her eyes dart around the image. My Dad lit the fire and blamed it on Gary, Dad adds. Nod, nod, nod. The reeds exploded, the flames moved so fast, and the heat was intense... so Gary took off in the opposite direction... Nod, nod, nod...

My parents have formed one of their reminiscence cocoons. I watch and listen to them play memory ping-pong. We were fishing in the creek, remember? And as I recall, we saw a red-bellied black snake slithering out of the reeds when they lit up... Gary wasn't the only one making a quick exit... An eventful day... It seems like yesterday... When was that again..?

———

'We die. We die, and we decay. We don't live on...' Simon Stone's film *The Dig* (2021) reimagines the 1939 excavation of Sutton Hoo in Suffolk, England, where a ship full of medieval artifacts and treasures was buried. Near the film's end, the landowner, Edith Pretty, her death imminent, chokes back tears. Basil Brown, whom Pretty had hired to oversee the excavation, responds: 'From the first human handprint on a cave wall, we're part of something continuous. So, we don't really die.'

A photograph is forever at risk of loneliness, being left in the dark where it can't be seen and must talk itself to sleep. Eyes render a photograph meaningful. I think of dirt as one of the few things that holds time. More than holds: cradles. Dirt is cooling, so we throw it on campfires to extinguish them. It smothers flames by blocking the oxygen, whereas memory, which is warming, is what we throw onto photographs. Memory: the smoldering mother of pictures.

I will be cremated, thank you, Auntie Mary announces. She snatches the photo of Gary and stares at it for so long that I wonder if she's had a stroke. Soil's too damn cold for my bones, she eventually says. There's no point in being a stiff flirt in the dirt.

I nod.

Mum nods.

Dad looks at the dirt under his right thumbnail.

Mum keeps a fireproof, light-tight pouch behind Dad's bucket of solder flux next to the door linking her kitchen to his garage, inside which swims spare credit cards, jewelry, passports, birth certificates, and childhood knickknacks. I don't know if I should be troubled (or even care) that there isn't a single photograph in it.

Light-tightness. A feature, a liability, of every photograph, every lost memory, every casket we bury.

As Mum and Dad pass the photograph of Uncle Gary between them, I notice the date on the back: December 15, 1973, exactly three years before Gary's life support machine was switched off.

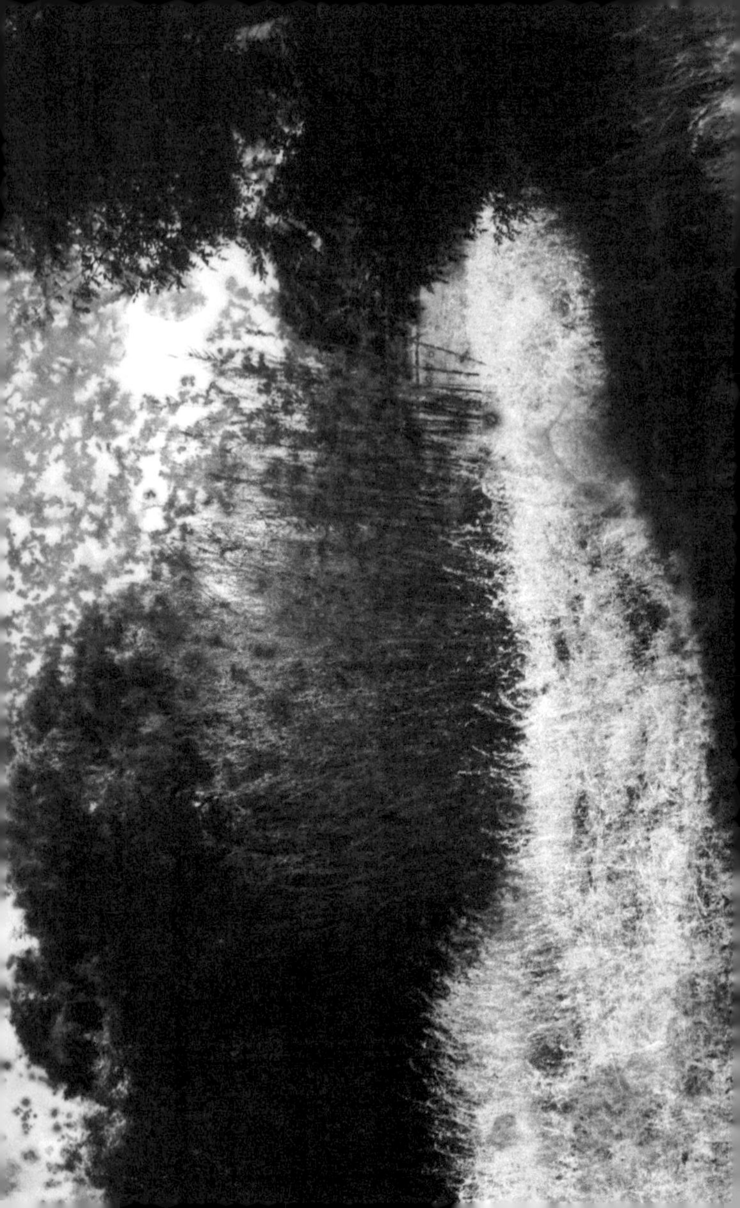

VII

Black and white and red
(and brown and blue) all over

The Other Colin's wheat farm is the place for spotlighting: startling rabbits with a 6,500-lumen Xenon-bulb light source. Dad brings his guns: Papa .308, mama .308, the Browning 10 automatic—shotty, shitty shotty, and baby shotty. The Other Colin drives like Xander Cage, rabbits dart and duck like Xiang. Afterward, the men divide the catch—these rabbits for stew, those for the dogs—and skin, gut, and clean the carcasses, except the ones with myxomatosis, a fatal disease introduced in Australia, Chile, and France in the 1950s to curb wild rabbit populations. Supper follows in Auntie Pam's kitchen. She serves sausage rolls and strawberry tarts decorated with X's made from hand-rolled pastry strips.

You'd think that the teenager who learned to drive her father's truck at age nine would remember all the tricks to navigating an extra-dewy dirt road. Alas, I am eager to escape my babysitting job. I brake too hard and lose control of Mum's white Ford Laser. It rolls four times before stopping upside down, headlights aglare. Much of the next hour is a bleary-blue blur. At the hospital, as Old Doc Tommo Junior sews the wound above my left index finger, I am questioned by a police officer checking his way down an official form with an official black clicky pen. Have you been drinking? No. Cross. *Click*. Are you wearing contact lenses? Yes. Check. *Click*. Pregnant that you know of? No (and I would know, thank you). Cross. *Click, click*. (Where inside our bodies do all our yeses and nos hang out?) Officer Clicky shines a torch in my eyes and watches my pupils do whatever they do after a car accident. Her night vision is a bit shit, Dad tells him, and she doesn't know her left from her right, just like her mother. Officer Clicky scribbles something in the notes section. *Click, click, click.* Old Doc Tommo Junior snatches and stuffs the pen into his white lab coat pocket. You're a lucky chook, he says to me.

Government-run crash marker programs aim to raise road safety awareness in rural areas by identifying the locations of severe and fatal car accidents. Wooden guideposts, painted black or red and marked with a white light-reflective symbolic cross, are fixed into the ground. My accident isn't considered 'severe,' so there's no such marker, except for a small X-shaped white scar on my finger. Today, I noticed for the first time that I press the X key with that finger to toggle between black and white in Adobe Photoshop.

Two painted X's mark the approximate spots where, on November 22, 1963, John F. Kennedy was fatally shot on Elm Street in Dallas,

Texas. Today, visitors wait for a gap in traffic, hurry to one of the X's to take a picture, and leave before more cars arrive. In 2013 the photographer Joachim Schmid positioned a webcam in a window on the sixth floor of the former Texas School Book Depository, where the assassin allegedly fired the shots. The webcam's perspective matches that of the killer, shooting tourists shooting memorial photos. It's a shrewd if morbid project about how and where we take pictures, oxymoronic behavior, and how easy it is to be Pavloved: the white X's on the pavement are the bell (or the clicky pen), and snap-happy tourists are the dogs, drooling at the thought of getting the ultimate shot.

If X marks the spot, initials mark the man. Would Kennedy be as memorable without the F.? Seven consecutive American presidents used a middle initial. Baby Boomers use them more than Gen Xers, who use them more than Millennials. The American television writer David X. Cohen assigned himself a new middle initial, replacing

S. with X. after encountering a computer system that couldn't distinguish between identical names. Malcolm X took the letter X for his unknown African name. When he declared publicly that JFK's assassination was an example of 'chickens coming home to roost' – a violent society suffering the consequences of violence – the religious leader Elijah Muhammad, Malcolm's mentor, ordered him to observe ninety days of silence. That was his quiet time.

Mum takes four photographs of her white Ford Laser at the scrapyard with her Pentax. Those four rectangular pieces of me live inside a white shoebox in Mum's pantry, along with a brown paper bag of glass shards Mum picked out of my hair. She implores me to revisit the site of my car accident and take photographs for closure. It's fifteen years before I succumb and borrow Dad's truck on a dazzling core-of-the-sun day. Daisies do the hokey-pokey in the wind. Bees kiss the fuzzy ears of stray barley on the roadside. The smell of bloodwood sap and quarry rock corroborates with memory: this is the place.

I find the offending curve and walk around it in a triangle. Then I plop myself among the daisies. Sitting with my new friends, my mind drifts to Richard Long's *England 1968*, for which he picked daisies along two lines to form an X in a field filled with them. The work only existed until the flowers grew again, but Long made a permanent record in the form of a photograph. He rearranged place, and in time, his rearrangement was reabsorbed by it.

Photography is often at the mercy of the prefix 're-,' I tell the daisies. They bob their frilly heads. Today, you are revisiting the blue of history, the daises reply, but remember, history isn't about providing answers. It's about providing context.

I pick a barley stalk and suck on it until my cheeks ache.

I thank the daisies for their candor.

'Anyone who has been there knows that the return home is never without pain,' writes Carol Mavor in *Blue Mythologies: Reflections on a Colour.* What colors braid home and pain? The color looking through the windshield of Dad's truck, freckled with bug bodies and bird shit; fatality brown, chlamydia green, gangrene green. In the distance, post-traumatic flashes of expulsion blue.

I could have sat in this mirage for an hour, four, or more. I didn't mark the time. I realized this was not a memory I wanted to remake. Today's memory, yes, but not the yesterday of fifteen years ago. It was all I could do to expose a roll of ghosts. By accident, that's precisely what I did. My camera heard and honored my wish. Every frame was overexposed.

Fall 2020, a bored-blue day. I make an appointment to see Old Doc Tommo Junior under the auspices of needing my constellations of mocha moles and habanero pepper freckles checked. He has 'really' on repeat as I recount the details of my car accident. He prods, scratches my skin, scratches his chin, umming and erring his way around my creasy, creaky body, occasionally pulling his glasses down, up, down, up his Germanic nose. Can he detect the crisscross of old aches? Funny, I don't remember any of that, he says. Oh well. He gives the examination table two affectionate slaps. You're all set, chook.

I drive to the car crash site and use my phone to take boring photographs of Then's leftovers. It's not the same; nor am I. The daisies are gone. The road is no longer covered in fine white gravel. Years of complaints about its lack of traction mean it's now surfaced in forget-about-it asphalt blue.

Chickens are night blind, so they come home to roost and, unlike me as a child, are content sleeping in a dark coop. Cows, meanwhile, can see in the dark better than humans, thanks to a light-reflecting surface called *tapetum lucidum*. They also have 330-degree vision and see every color except for red. No chicken breed names start with the letter X, but in cows, there is Xinjiang Brown, a sort of honey biscuit, Mother

Hubbard's cupboard brown. Dad harrumphs. That's not a real cow; it's a crossbreed.

When Mum and Dad moved to our farm in 1973, every room had an accent wall. Brother BJ's was the reddest, between Happy Christmas red and Tarantino red. Mum gives a little shiver. That's where Old Mrs. Evans's son Thomas killed himself with his father's Iver Johnson Model X action rifle, Dad says. Consequently, Old Mrs. Evans's daughter, Sister Joan, visits yearly, wearing her brown and white habit. Always uninvited, Dad says. Yes, always out-of-the-blue, Mum agrees. She'd step out of the car, kneel, kiss the ground three times, then take out her holy water and draw crosses on each side of the farmhouse.

When Dad's bank loan to buy the farm is approved, Old Mrs. Evans moves out of the cottage next door. She leaves behind the heavy cotton floral drapes—which Mum von Trapps into dresses for me—plus a few paintings, mismatched crockery, and canned goods. Years later, Dad is replacing floor joists and finds an envelope with a stained, underexposed 4x5 film negative of his dairy under construction. It is his favorite photograph to this day.

Red is only black remembering—the first line of Ocean Vuong's poem, "Daily Bread." I think about Dad's negative hiding under the floorboards, waiting to become a photograph. What color is the unknown, the misremembered, the forgotten? The shade of black inside the camera—wait, is it black? I abandon my computer, let my body sink into the comfiest part of Dad's brown sofa, and mentally navigate a Rothko road from blackish to outer space to raisin, a splotch of merlot, tinge of burgundy, grids of aggressive tartan, to the horizon of a sunset bruise. Onyx, off-black, black olive black, long black coffee black, blackout blind black? Betrayal-black, inside a safe black?

A color called Xiketic.

You'd never know from their mouths that my grandmothers attended church. Nan E. swore nonstop. Nana L. was a serial blasphemer. And Lord, they had their tics. Each kept a wall calendar, which small-town butchers gave to loyal customers. Nan E., left-handed, hung her calendar to the left of the red telephone on Grandpa's brown desk. She marked off each day with an X, using her favorite slut-red-dress red marker, one of many before-bed rituals. During the summer holidays, I'd catch her making those two quick strokes as if expelling the last sins of the day. Nana L., right-handed, hung hers to the right of the good-news-blue wall-mounted telephone in the hallway. She favored ripping the perforated sheets as deftly as the bad-luck letter X pages from the telephone directory. Fifty-three years' worth of pages I wish I'd collected.

Photographers have rituals for yessing their pictures. Some use dots, stars, or hashes. Others circle the desired frame. The photographer Marc Elliott draws little X's in pencil (which he later erases) on the back of the darkroom prints he considers final. In *7 Original Contact Sheets of Interior Details in Walker Evans's Apartment*, the 'good' frames are outlined in red while the 'bad' ones are crossed out with X's.

Crossing out can indicate a new beginning. In the face of a copyright bill that would retroactively erase a trove of photographs of the Argentine dictatorship from the public domain, the artist Stephanie Mercedes manipulated the images through layering, cropping, and Xing them, thus gaining the legal rights to copyright the altered images and re-donate them. Without Mercedes' intervention, the Argentine people would have lost access to their traumatic history. William Klein conceived of his series *Painted Contacts* while reviewing other photographers' contact sheets for a movie he was making. Noticing how they marked 'good' images from 'bad' ones, Klein defiled his own contact sheets with X's, using brushstrokes of bright enamel paint, thus reframing and refocusing the viewer's gaze on the essential photographic processes of editing and selection.

Thomas Barrow went a step further for his series *Cancellations* (1973-1981), carving X's onto his negatives of grungy, desolate American spaces. Today, I am looking at *Dart* (1974). The photograph is taken looking up at big storm clouds. A giant arrow appears to have plunged from them. In the background are various stores: K-Mart, Snappy Photos, and Goodwill. Crossing out the scene is a big, beautiful X. It's almost comical. How much goodwill exists in permanently damaging a silver nitrate surface? But then, is it really 'damaging'? Barrow's act considers the making and arranging of a photograph and self-vandalism. He makes an ordinary scene extraordinary with the simplest of marks. Some look neat and polite, others rageful. If we think of the negative as a piece of the dead, Barrow's X-mark is a kind of gestural resuscitation, an exception to the Do Not Resuscitate clause imposed by the camera. Maybe less DNR and more CNR (Can Not Resituate): after all, we can't revive that which has never known breath.

I get sidetracked, wondering if Barrow is left- or right-handed. Left-handers write some letters differently from right-handers because they find it easier to move their pens in a counterclockwise direction. I clear Mum's kitchen table for an experiment. Mum, right-handed, writes her letter X in ballot style. Auntie Mary, also right-handed, forms hers more in the Greek style than in the Latin style. My left-handed daughter carves her X's in swift strokes like Zorro. Dad refuses to participate.

I re-examine Barrow's photographs, and though I can tell which stroke was made first, I can't determine from which direction. 'Right-handed,' Tom confirms by email. 'When I began, I remember trying to be consistent with going from corner to corner. As time passed, I often went over the strokes more than once and flipped the negative as the emulsion side made a different mark than the uncoated side.' He, too, became fascinated by the letter X. 'One that stuck in my mind was in one of the biographies of Nathanael West, a photo of a canceled page from *The Day of the Locust,* with a corner-to-corner X. Very physical and a 'new' object.'

George Eastman may have wanted to put photography in the hands of anyone who could press a button, but I don't think he considered handedness. It wasn't until 1994 that Kodak filed a patent for switchable camera functions for right-hand and left-hand user-activated controls. To this day, there are almost no left-handed cameras. An exception is the Exakta, produced by Ihagee Kamerawerk in Dresden, a variant of which—the VX—is used by Jimmy Stewart's character in Alfred Hitchcock's *Rear Window*. Stewart plays Jeff, a wheelchair-bound professional photographer who spends his days spying on his possibly murderous neighbor.

It's the same with guns, says Dad. Your grandmother tried to shoot your grandfather several times, but her leftness got in the way. He shakes his head at me, implying some fault on my part. 'Cross him out and hope he dies.' That's what she used to say! He looks to Mum for validation. She busies herself with Operation Tidiness.

Sometimes, Odette, your grandmother was a real bitch.

Later, Nan. E's cross-him-out-hope-he-dies is on replay as I look out the window where the moon is bent like a fishhook. I don't recall seeing a single photograph of Nan E. and Grandpa together, not on the walls, mantles, or in our albums. When they married in 1937, there was no photographer. Whatever love they had or hoped to hold is photographically non-existent.

Grandpa once said that the camera was a prism, but it occurs to me only now I may have heard *prism* in place of *prison*.

Something old, something new, something borrowed, something blue, someone blue, or somewhere blue. I watch the moon liquesce behind the rain. When Judy Garland sang "Somewhere Over the Rainbow," in addition to looking for a place where she wouldn't get into trouble, I like to think she was looking for her particular blue beyond the rain. Pinafore blue, pigtail ribbon blue, studio light highlights on the Tin Man's costume blue. Not indigo, more teal-ish, cyan-ish, different to the blue Isaac Newton saw in his rainbow, which was more violet, more *roses are red, violets are blue* blue.

Spectrum, continuum, 'ishy' nouns for a rainbow. And wedlock.

'Always be sure to get your moon in the right part of the sky.' The author Eudora Welty took this advice from a critic to heart, a reminder that small details, even *ish* ones, matter.

Tonight, my moon illuminates copper-bodied moths pancaking on the wall, a different moon from the one that once globed Old Jack Adams sitting in his porch rocker, smoking a pipe of regrets, reading porn tucked inside his battered Old Farmer's Almanac. I try to fall sleep with the sound of the river *ishing* into my room, over Mum's sewing machine, over the white duvet, over my eyes. I look out again and mentally pin in a cute factoid I'd almost forgotten: the hand gesture for signing a letter X in American Sign Language involves sticking out your index finger and bending it into a hook.

Our faces are brokers of what's happening inside our bodies, just as our eyes are proverbial 'windows to the soul.' I rewatch *Rear Window* and copy into my notebook something that Stella, the visiting nurse, says to Jeff: 'We've become a race of Peeping Toms. What people ought to do is get outside their own house and look in for a change.' Yes. We see and feel things differently when we leave the comfort or confines of what we know. When we look through a camera, we change the things we observe. I stand up, walk outside, set my camera on a tripod, and look. The glass of Mum's kitchen window is duller, the reflections milkier. I notice the cracked vinyl on the armrest of Dad's brown chair and the sallow of Mum's refrigerator.

I have a theory about looking. *Thin* looking is akin to looking through a window. There's a frame and a veneer between me and the world, but what's outside is so vast, so abundant, so never-ending-story that it offers ample space for the thick feelings inside me to race. *Thick* looking is like looking at a photograph, which, although a thin object, has density and often feels impenetrable to me, even if the content is minimal (actually, especially if it's minimal). I have to empty my mind to let this thickness of content in.

A view can expand our vision but also hold us back, restricting or narrowing our interests. Looking through a window, viewfinder, scope, or magnifier—or at a photograph, for that matter—it's easy to become locked into a singular way of thinking at the expense of looking at and thinking about other things. At the cost of deeper feelings, higher steps.

I return to my computer and cycle through fonts that begin with the letter X: Xantorid, Xomai,

Xecrian, Xiano, and my favorite, Xwisth, for how it sounds—*xwisthy*. In typography, the x-height or corpus size refers to the height of the lowercase x for a typeface. When the x-height is large, the typeface is probably easier to read at small sizes. Why x? Because her body lacks curves. X is easy to measure and place, as easy as a-b-c.

After staring into the lexis too long, I click on X to close the active window.

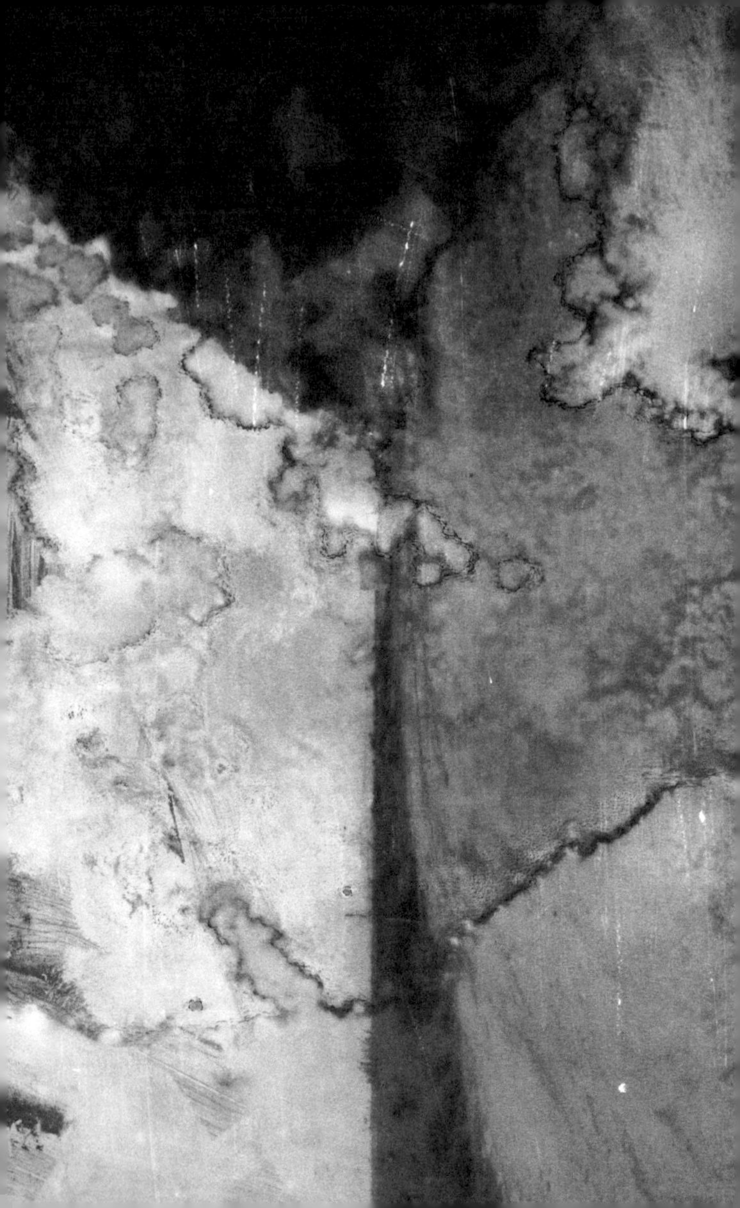

VIII

Xanax, pissing about

Dad loved boozing. Photography let the bottle out of the bag. Hidden in a box of tarnished football trophies and tatty report cards are five color Polaroids of Dad playing late-night drinking games with his twentysomething buddies Brian, Bert, and Richard on the old ferry. The too-harsh flash denies details while illuminating others. The men have sideburns and wonky facial expressions, heightened by the wonky angles at which the unknown photographer holds the camera. Each gives a thumbs-up with their left hand while clutching the longnecks of XXXX in their right. I count nineteen empty XXXX bottles lined up along the ferry railing in one picture. These glossy translations of good times confirm the excess of beer that leaves Dad with rollercoaster rows of X and Y scars where his appendix was removed, then his gall bladder, then part of his spleen. Three scars, you're out, Old Doc Tommo Senior tells Dad. You have to stop pissing around. Dad laughs. Did I give a Fourex? Of course, I fucking didn't.

XXXX—pronounced Fourex—is a beer brewed by Castlemaine Perkins. Cheap shit, tasted like piss, recalls Dad. Introduced in 1924, the name XXXX harks to a long tradition of using Xs to denote the strength of an ale. More Xs meant a higher alcohol content. Some believe the X mark originates from the breweries of medieval monasteries, where X guaranteed quality. Another explanation relates to the excise duty on alcoholic beverages beginning in England in 1643. An X mark on a case of beer indicated that its contents were stronger than legal small beer limits and thus subject to a tax of ten shillings per barrel. Later, brewers added additional X marks to signify stronger beers.

Your father drank four or five longnecks every night, Mum says, glancing at Dad. He's watching TV, gripped by an ad for sprinklers. He gave away drinking when we got together, and the guys were unhappy – 'under the thumb,' they said. She lowers her voice. It was frustrating. I tell Mum about Socrates' wife, Xanthippe, who became so irritated with him that one day she dumped the contents of a chamber pot over his head. Mum wrinkles her nose. Nan E. cheers from six feet below.

Amy Levy, a 19th-century British writer, published a poem in 1881 called "Xantippe," spelled without the 'h,' which tells the story from a different perspective. Levy paints a picture of Xantippe as a woman enraged by Socrates' dismissal of her intelligence. This version of Xantippe admires Socrates for his mind and ideas but is devastated to learn he doesn't feel the same way.

You married me for my mind, didn't you, darlin'? asks Dad. Mum tumbleweeds a reply.

Alcoholism runs deep on Dad's side of the family. His maternal grandfather Gustav is drunk when he registers Nan E.'s birth. Rather than the agreed name Dora-Bella, she is called Xarella, and everyone thinks she is named after worming medicine. Nan E. shortens it to Rella, the meaning of which in Old German is, incredibly, 'other, foreign.' Upon her marriage to Grandpa, Nan E. asks the registry to change her name, but for unknown reasons, is refused, so she crosses out the 'Xa,' leaving 'rella' on her birth certificate, and, in the process, invalidates it. From that moment, as far as the registry is concerned, Nan E. has no legal existence.

X may be the only alphabet letter to make us stand out *and* eliminate us.

After Nan. E's father is beheaded in a car accident, her mother suffers long bouts of depression and is later diagnosed with an inoperable tumor.

She accepts recommendations by the Old Duck Club after church, gorging on their tales of medical marvels as if they're gospel. Try this ointment, says Duck One. No, no, no, you need to add yeast, Duck Two insists. Nonsense, that won't help, says Duck Three. Do you know Howard Schultz? He was diagnosed with cancer, and he took a dose of that Compound X stuff, and it was magic. She leans in closer. He passed the foulest stools, but all the cancer came out, and when the doctors took X-rays, the growth was gone! Gasps all around. That's all very well, pips Duck Four, but my cousin's friend's brother had a big, giant, enormous cancerous mole on his neck, and he used that X lotion, which burnt his skin clean off, but the cancer went away...

The filename for my manuscript is 'LetterX_AutoSave.' I should rename it, but the AutoSave part reminds me to back up daily after my laptop crashes. Oh, the terror of losing data and then—hurrah! It comes back. The best-ever kind of back, not the-cancer-is-back or that immortal line from

The Terminator I'll-be-back, or *Back to the Future* back. My document is saved, sort of. There is the odd missing word and Wingdings character, but mostly, I am back to normal, back on track. Better yet, I am auto-back. Who needs a cyborg or a DeLorean when you have time machine-like functionality built into your software? Thank you, AutoSave. Thank you, anxiety-reduction pills.

Hundreds of drugs start with or include the letter X. Xanax, made by Pfizer, is the only one that starts and ends with X (and one of many drug names that is a palindrome). There's even a phonetically clever X-named drug for treating dry eye disease called Xiidra (pronounced z-eye-drah), often prescribed to photographers. Bizarrely, its main side effects include blurred vision and eye irritation, for which you might then need Ocu-dex, Lotemax, or Maxitrol. If your dry eyes create too many tears—a condition called reflex tearing—another X drug is available. That's a lot of X's for nixing problem peepers.

3 p.m., annual eye exam. I pay closer-than-usual attention to the letters on the Snellen Eye Chart. There are no X's on it, and Dr. Scott says I won't find any on the Bailey-Lovie chart or newer LogMAR charts, either. 'X is excluded because it's unique,' he says. 'B's can look like E's, and D's can look like O's, but X is a one-off. Can you read the letter at the top for me, please?'

'X,' I joke.

When an XL Falcon clips Dad's bike in December 1964, his first pair of glasses is smashed, and he loses nine teeth. He hates the dentist's drill and, the idiot that he is, opts to have his remaining teeth extracted. Months later, he can't stop showing off his dentures. He makes up for his lack of smarts with the county's whitest smile and a superhuman ability to be charming. Not Prince Charming charming or 'Bond, James Bond' charming but hooligan-daredevil charming and everything the fifteen-year-old girl who would become my mother wanted. Dad had a lot of ex-girlfriends, but Mum became his Agent XXX, star of *The Would-Be Farmer Who Loved Me.*

My exes are photographs *sous-viding* in my basement. J. is the only one who occasionally pops into mind. He was an alcoholic, as was his father, robbed of his medical practice and then life at age 47. J. inherits the house and keeps a framed black-and-white photograph of his dad, deliriously Cary Grant handsome, on his bedside table. I remember daydreaming into that picture, asking it questions like a Magic 8 Ball (I already knew the answers but refused to acknowledge them even after three years). The last time I saw J. was in 2009. I can still see regret hoisting the corners of his mouth, the surplus of blue and red spider veins protruding from the skin around his nose and cheeks. When I try to track him down online in a late-night fit of longing, he is Xed out of existence. Our relationship is forever a dog-eared, whiskey-stained, haphazardly taped, unframed shade of love that lost its way to the chapel.

My first taste of alcohol coincides with my townie friend H. sneaking a bootleg copy of *Penthouse* to school along with a water bottle filled with gin. We duck into the toilet block at lunchtime. H. pulls both items from her backpack. We sit on the tiled floor of a single stall, taking turns swigging while examining vaginas, explosions of semen, and ads endorsing Forex lambskin condoms over latex ones. Our eyes are trapped in a labyrinth of lust, so much so that we don't notice the door opening. S., a classmate, looks down at us in shock. I immediately stand and zip my fly, which is wide open because I'm fat. S. tells everyone we're lesbians. It's the better story because H. is tall, blonde, and everything I am not. When H. comes to stay at our farm, she spends most of her time ogling the men working topless outdoors. Years later, I heard that H. changed her name to Virginia Vixen and acted in a series of taboo-blue movies.

The Motion Picture Association of America classification system, implemented in 1968, originally consisted of four ratings: G for general audiences, M for mature, R for restricted, and X for over sixteens only. The X rating is where it all went wrong: it wasn't trademarked like the others, which meant 'X' could stand for more than a naughty film. It could stand for movies that were sexy, dangerous, and exploitative. It could stand for those with an *excess* of sex, danger, and exploitation. Film distributors preyed on this lack of a clear definition, adding XX and then XXX to mean extreme sex, danger, and exploitation. *Midnight Cowboy*, the first and only X-rated Academy Award winner for Best Picture, initially rated R, was changed to an X rating due to the film's homosexual references and depiction of violent gang rape.

X NOTE
The abbreviation for a medical prescription is Rx, which in Latin means 'to take,' a phrase synonymous with photography, alcohol, pharmaceuticals, and violence: *to take* a photograph, *to take* a drink or pill, *to take* without permission, *to take* a life.

Xanax axes anxiety. When you take the 'x' out of anxiety, you get aniety, which sounds calmer. I type aniety into Google. Did you mean anxiety? Did you mean ancient? The italics and under-lining are anxiety-inducing. Google directs me to Amazon, where the word anxiety is misspelled for a book titled *Healing Fear: New Approaches to Overcoming Aniety* (since corrected, but I have a screenshot, ha!) There's even a bonafide fear of the letter X, Xinoaphobia, for which the treatment is antidepressants, tranquilizers, or beta-blockers. What strikes me is how someone with Xinoaphobia would read about their condition. One article I read contains seventy mentions of the letter X.

There was slow-growing cancer on our farm, a long-hand form of anxiety in Dad's logbooks. It was in the slumping of parental shoulders, the muffled phone calls and dead-air stares through net curtains, in the visits from city folks wearing cheap suits and knockoff eau de sincerity. There was no quick fix for my longing, no cute barrettes for pulling back the front pieces of memory, no needle and thread for taking up the hems of heartbreak. I saw a lot and heard a lot, but an apple a day of Mum's reassurances kept my worry at bay. I remember playing *Monopoly* with Dad in those later years, after milking, as the crescents of his eyes waned. He was always the car, I the top hat. Pass go, he'd say, but you might as well forget the two hundred dollars. It's nowhere near enough.

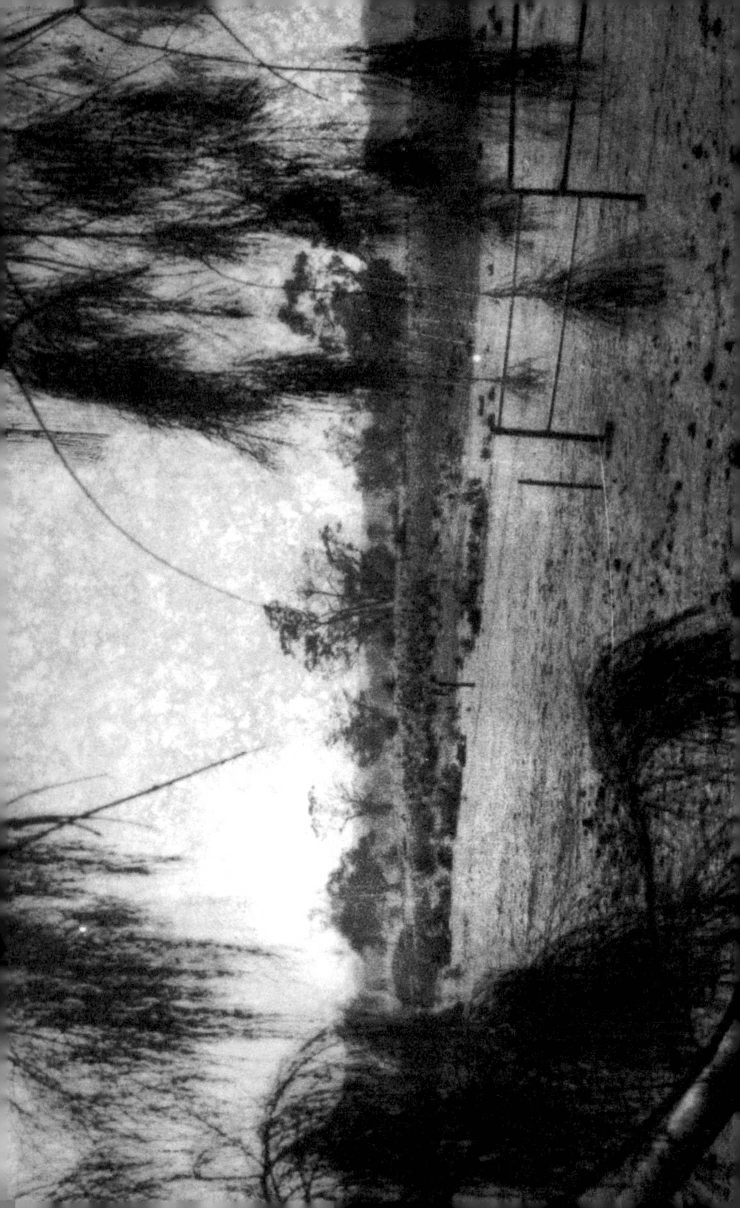

IX

Null-forgiving operator

The emotional synthetics who buy our farm don't have cows, goldfish, or even a pet rock. They intend to use it as a hobby farm, says Wilkie the Accountant. It will become a place of recreation, run at an ongoing loss (*how to outrun loss*) — a 'lifestyle choice' for unnecessary knitting projects, quaint geraniums, and prisons for tomatoes. Dad and Mum spend hours in Wilkie's city-air-conditioned office. Brother BJ and I wait in the waiting room. He plays with LEGO while I sulk into a Nancy Drew mystery, praying for the Hardy Boys to jump off the page and solve *The Hex of the Disappearing Farm*.

On our last visit to Wilkie's office, Dad parks his Falcon near the front door, and we all pitch in to unpack the final consignment of boxed financial records and assemble them into an ugly fort in the waiting room. I adjust my mopey pants and drop into the chair next to a fake ficus. I'm too young to understand and too old to play. Once upon a time, a box was an object of excitement and promise. In their empty state, they held all the potential in the world. These boxes are not those boxes. These bothering brown coffins are the reality of a use-by, sell-by, bye-bye date.

After several unacknowledged huffs and silly thumb-sucks, I remove one of the rubbing-me-the-wrong-way HANDLE WITH CARE stickers and slap it hard on my chest. Oops. Up comes the five slices of homemade pizza I'd eaten on our drive to the city. Dad berates Mum for leaving the dairy bucket in the back seat.

Xerography is a dry photocopying technique invented in 1938 by the American physicist Chester

Carlson. It wasn't until 1960 that a fully automated process for copying became a reality with the release of the Xerox 914. Photographers and other artists didn't wait long to try this new mass-production technology. Laurie-Rae Chamberlain, a punk-inspired color Xeroxer, began exhibiting her experiments in the mid-1970s. Joan Semmel's working process included using a color Xerox machine to create collages for her paintings, including her 1977 oil-on-canvas *Central X*. Helen Chadwick photocopied her own body, nude, and used it as subject matter for *Labours I-X* and *The Oval Court* (1986).

Copies of copies on reflex paper, umpteen sign here, there, everywhere. My parents signed away their livelihood in time with the *hweeeclick-aschmunggg–thwip* of Wilkie's Xerox machine. I'm hypnotized by the strip of light moving back and forth over the glass horizon. I channel Auntie Mary and try to think of seven-letter words to make out of hypnosis. After an hour, all I've come up with is sonship, the relationship between a son and father. Dad shakes hands with Wilkie for the last time. There's a pause in his usually swift grip. He looks at Brother BJ sitting on the floor, deep in some stand-off situation with a LEGO enemy. It could not be a sadder or more accurate reflection of the real-life drama playing in Wilkie's office. We all know that Dad wanted to give our farm to Brother BJ one day.

On the long drive home, Mum tries to reassure us that living on a townie-sized block of land will be a mini-version of our farm and that all we have to do is use our imagination. Dad's eyes don't leave the road. I'm capital-D Dying to object, but I sense now is not the time; there will never be a time, and things will never be the same as they ever were. We travel the remaining seventy miles in blunted blue silence. Dad's Falcon, lightened from unloading fiscal tumors, is heavier than ever.

1995, SIX YEARS POST-SALE

An early summer evening of grasshoppers

and featherlight, perfect for a drive-by, just me and my bluebird-blue Datsun Bluebird. The light, *that light*, was the high point. Do you know That Light? The light we get two, three, sometimes four times a year after a late afternoon downpour? The light that leans into *-ish*: butterfly-wing-ish, amaryllis-ish, yellow-brick-road-ish. *That Light*. But even with these golden rods of God, everything looks worn and tired, especially the lone farmer wearing donkeywork blue overalls, forking hay from one pile to another. He looks straight at me. I look straight back. We are gently curious about each other. For a second, he seems afraid. I feel a perforation. Then it's gone — ghost pain.

Driving and looking, looking for squints of familiarity. Uprooted FOR SALE signs dot the roadside. The swamps, usually thick with clover, are tinged with blasphemous and belligerent browns. I wind down the window a bit further — the scent of plums. Calves cry. Crickets chafe. The occasional *moo* makes me feel gooey. Pulling up at the end of our driveway, the goo turns to slush. Our homestead looks wobbly, all the sheds and fences Dad built, even the gates with big double X cross braces. Or maybe that's just me.

I climb atop one of the gates and look towards the river. The letter X has an extraordinary relationship with space. She is linear, perpendicular, and graphic. She can extend her arms and legs in four directions to emphasize and exaggerate distance. Looking at a pyramid or obelisk from above, it forms an X in a box—isn't that something? In every index, dictionary, and telephone directory, X occupies the least space yet is the star of a dizzying array of functions and purposes. This breadth of versatility makes all the other letters seem mundane. They say size doesn't matter, but the letter X suggests it does. In Roman numerals, X denotes the number 10; with a horizontal line drawn above it, it means 10,000.

Measurements didn't matter when Dad cut wire to repair his fences or when Mum needed to triple the ingredients for her blueberry cobbler. But boy, did they matter for Dad's overalls, and only one brand, color, and size were worthy: Hard Yakka Bib & Brace, khaki, 44. When alpha-sizing was developed in 1996, Dad was pissed. Sizes ranged from XXS to XXXL, the idea being that letter coding would simplify and standardize the production process. Extra Xs have since been added. We now have XXXSP (extra, extra, extra small petite) through to XXXXL-XLx2 (extra, extra, extra, extra, large, extra-long, times two).

2005, SIXTEEN YEARS POST-SALE

I coax Mum to join me. The latest owner of our farm, Steve the Expat, spends half the year in Thailand and the other half driving a road train from coast to coast. Yeah, visit whenever you want, Steve tells Dad on the phone. Mind the dogs. When Mum and I arrive, a Red Heeler and Labrador retriever lick us near clean. I spend hours taking photographs and instruct Mum to do the same. I return a few months later with negatives and bury them deep in the soil. I attach some to trees and dilapidated buildings. It's a flawed, inexact process, just like me.

Harvest season. I reap and sow negatives. It's an ongoing ritual, a labor of love and loss (often of XXL sacrifice and XXS reward), observing a landscape of pain and focussing on its scars. It's also a photographic autopsy of my relationship to a place I still call home but where I no longer live. A place I hold still, even as that phrase causes my mind to gallop. The performance continues. I leave my negatives for the dark to devour, and every time I return, I self-erase a bit more of what I hold dear. I tell myself that process isn't the answer and that the thing, the photograph, contributes an answer by coming into being. I am the old and the restless, the director and producer, down to my fingertips and shadow. With every look, every attempt at *this photograph*, I objectify her body and soak mine in overall blue.

2018, TWENTY-NINE YEARS POST-SALE

My less-fit legs gauge the length of Dad's paddocks, trying to locate the hundreds of negatives and prints I've buried. A swell of haptic, disorienting experiences come hell or high river. I am waist-deep in melancholy. I thought that by now, I'd have generated enough neutralizing antibodies against the pox of nostalgia. Alas, there are always new infections. Photographs rent memory, and memory is a lousy tenant. I say out loud for the first time the phrase that proves you're not getting old, you're already there: *I'm getting old.* Everything is becoming 'used to.' This used to be easier. It used to be fun.

Found one! There is the occasional successful exhumation. But mostly, our farm refuses to divulge her belly full of my silver treasures. She claims them as her own, protecting the border between the world of living color above and monochrome below. I had hoped to retrieve more negatives by now to look at our farm anew. I had hoped for a posthumous breath of fresh air. *I had hope.* I find five negatives over the next two years: split, cracked, and torn, all adjectives for broken. They are in sync with the botched blue of memory.

Moyra Davey writes of the compulsion to lose and find things. 'Lost and found is a ritual of redemption. If I find the thing, then I am a worthy person. I have been granted a reprieve. I have relief when I find something, but it's a shallow, superficial relief. I know this ritual is a rehearsal for all the inevitable, bigger losses. I think, if I can only find X, then I am holding back the floodwaters, I am in control.'

Maybe that's why I prefer broken stuff. If my pictures are broken, they understand loss. They understand me. I remember the photographer Ahndraya Parlato telling me that a competent photograph alone lacks soul. Indeed. For all its pros—good composition, check/cross, good lighting, check/cross, good exposure, check/cross—this con is big. This photograph never leaves the shallows of the good-enough river. *This photograph needs X*, a saturating combination of damaged somethings river-deep, mountain-high. Yeah, yeah, yeah.

Photography should involve purpose and drift. It sounded good when I wrote it in my notebook, but now it's a pain in my ass. I'm doing something with purpose, without any intention of it being good or bad, in a thirsty loam over which I have no control. I try to use my camera as a remedy for homesickness, among other ails, and it dispenses placebo pictures. I allow, invite, even force damage because I am damaged. I'm building a mirror.

I gingerly ask Nan. E. for advice. She *tsks* loud as a locust. You ate too much dirt as a child.

The photographer Stephen Mayes visits my studio to inspect prints I've made from some of my disentombed negatives. 'People love to recognize things in a photograph,' he says. 'If it's recognizable, it's relatable. And if it's human, it's very relatable.' We stare into the ruins. We talk about the radicalness of consciousness. 'These seem like interfaces between what's known and what's elsewhere,' he says, dipping his head back and forth from my prints like a drinking bird toy. 'I don't know if you're repeating memory, coercing it, kebabbing it, or submitting to it. They make me suspicious why you need photography to activate a sense of elsewhere.' He pauses and looks out the window, his eyes flicking between his reflection and the convoy of cars on the bridge. 'Perfection is death,' he says (whether to me, himself, or the world, I'm not sure). Once a circle is perfect, there's nothing to be touched, nothing to be done.

Come hell or high river. It means getting it done, no matter what. Dad says it often, less so as our farm years slide like mud into the river. He forgets it was a favorite phrase, even when I press him.

Some ancient Greeks believed that souls were forced to drink from the river before reincarnation so they wouldn't remember their past lives. The Myth of Er in Book X of Plato's *Republic* tells of the dead arriving at a barren waste called the Plain of Lethe through which the Ameles Potamos, or river of unmindfulness, runs. 'Of this, they were all obliged to drink a certain quantity,' Plato writes, 'and those who were not saved by wisdom drank more than was necessary; and each one as he drank forgot all things.'

I read this quote aloud. It is met with a muzzle. Mum wonders whether now is the right time to offer tea again. Auntie Mary, threading wands of wattle into an urn, cannot resist the XL silence. She recites an English riddle:

> X is a seven-letter word.
> X is impossible for God
> Newborns like X better than milk
> The poor have X, and the rich look for X
> from the poor
> If you eat X, you will die
> X is more important than your life
> I will give you X if you get the answer...

Nothing, my parents say in unison.

"X Stands for Nothing" is the name of episode 653 of *This Week in Tech*, an Apple podcast in which a roundtable of mostly men talks about tech trends. Brian X. Chen, the lead consumer technology writer for *The New York Times*, is a guest in this episode dedicated to Elon Musk, who may love the letter X more than anyone else. One of Musk's first start-ups? X.com. His rocket company? SpaceX. Tesla, of which he is CEO and the largest shareholder, manufactures the Model X, one of the world's best-selling plug-in cars. Even one of his sons bears the Mark of Musk: X Æ A-Xii.

Long before Musk's son, a child named X was raised as part of an experiment to keep its gender unknown to everyone but the parents and scientists. *X: A Fabulous Child's Story*, written by Lois Gould, was first published as a science fiction short story in 1972 and then a picture book in 1978. It touches on many topics encased in that thing X has down pat: meaning so much or nothing.

A photograph of nothing. What does it look like? I could try to use math or science to answer the question, *if X, then Y, where X is the cause of Y*, but I fear I'll enter a never-ending loop, like the chicken-egg paradox. In old naval slang, an X-chaser was good at math—someone gifted at working out the value of nothing. During the only recorded public address given by the artist Lutz Bacher—a pseudonym; she never publicly revealed a former name—she told a story about her teacher asking her to solve for X in front of the class. Bacher pretended to understand what X was so that she could sit down. I feel the same way, pretending to know what I'm talking about, about nothing, but coming up with—nothing.

Sheesh. 'Nothing' is hard to think about, let alone write about, since 'nothing' is neither cause nor effect. We can't fully explain many things—including the letter X, photographs, and memory—without cause and effect. And we can't un-see causal relations. We like relationships between things. When we can't explain something, we slap an X on top of it, in front of it, instead of it, or we have a nice cup of tea. Because causes, like photographs and memory, are too vague for a precise science. We can observe them to a point but can't measure them to the nth. They defy WYSIWYG (What You See Is What You Get).

Auntie Mary holds up her iPhone. Look, you can buy 'I Heart Elon' flags on eBay! My mind has moved on. I'm thinking about Stephen Hawking proclaiming heaven is a fairy story for people afraid of death because the idea of nothing after death is scary. I'm thinking about 'I Heart X!' as a team-building t-shirt for Musk's Musketeers and why there isn't a heart emoji with an X on top. Maybe too many photographs, like too many emojis, like too many X's, cancel themselves out and become equal to nothing, not even zero, the score given to an extinct species.

At this point of the philosophical pretzel, I hear the writer David Campany reminding me that a photograph belongs wherever we put it. It belongs everywhere and nowhere. It has no relationship to scale, materiality, support, season, society, or platform. It has no built-in vocabulary of its own. It has no beginning or end.

How do we know anything? Dad asks.

Unsettling thoughts. Sometimes, Dad will say something so chewy that it takes ages to swallow and won't siphon out of my system for months. Is there anything that means nothing, really real nothing? When something means nothing, we call it X. We turn it into a potent something. X fills the void to allow nothing to have meaning. Imagine discovering that nothing is as empty, sad, unfixed, or zilch-and-zippered as we think. As in "nothing's wrong" when everything seems wrong. What do you want? NOTHING (but we do). What can you do? NOTHING (but we can). Too often, we say 'nothing' when we don't know or don't want to know. There should be an X-word for that, surely.

The problem, my problem, is not X or photography or our farm or what happens when something is Xed out. These somethings will always carry a punctuated power. The problem, my problem, is that their twisty relationship is at once meaningful and hopeless. I am writing sensuous atmospheric camerawork about the dark, the light years of yesterday, overseeing (directing, examining), overlooking (forgetting, omitting), and the other overlooking (excusing, closing my eyes to). I am writing it with an irregular heartbeat to a malfunctioning metronome.

I am writing *grave.*

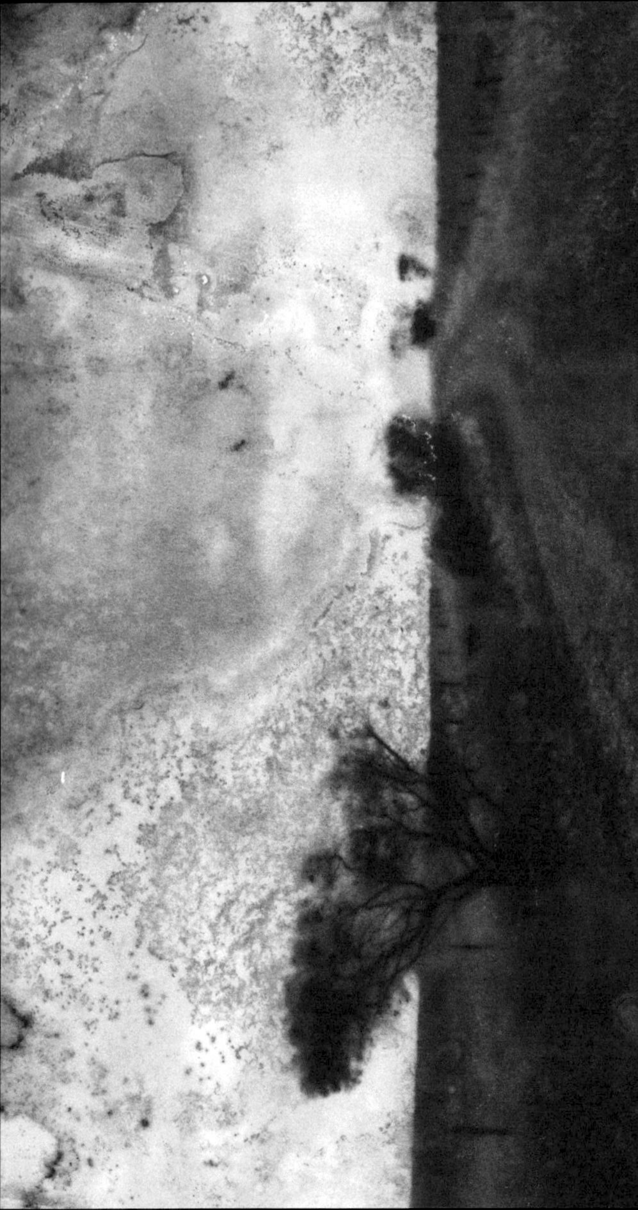

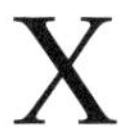

Exodus

Exodus is the only book in the Bible with the letter X in its name. Its abbreviation is Ex. I research the etymological root of exodus, and upon finding the answer, a wash of discomfort and irony covers my body. The word was adopted into English via Latin from the Greek *Exodus*, which means 'the road out.'

Silence befalls Mum's kitchen table. Dad slides Mum's butter dish five inches to his left. Auntie Mary fiddles with a speckled petal of a lily drooping in its vase. There are no more slaps, laughs, or digs. At last, X—the letter used to represent the unknown and the indescribable—pulls up a chair at our conversational fork in the road.

Welcome to the family.

It's amusing that once upon a time (the ultimate first line), X was deleted. In 1755, Samuel Johnson omitted it from his *Dictionary of the English Language*. In 2007, in Saudi Arabia, the Commission for the Promotion of Virtue and Prevention of Vice declared that because X looked like a cross, it was sinful. In Turkey, it was banned until 2013.

X NOTE
There are 853 X's in this book.

As the pause grows longer and more complex, I notice Dad's hands crossed before him. The essential knowledge and skill of the farmer, the embodied traditions stored in his muscles. His body knows and remembers many cycles of improvisation and repair. My love for the land came from a sun lit by him. My soft spot for reminiscence came from the gently leaking vessel of my mother's body. I cross my own hands as if ready to pray. I've been praying for 26,875 words. *Dear X, our phonetic chameleon. Hallowed be your name. You are the swish of intensifying static, the scrunch of cellophane. You are swords clashing, cats coughing, filets sizzling in Mum's frypan. You replicate various sounds—ks, gz, z, k, kzh—yet can hush up as in tableaux or choux pastry. X has no climax or ending. X who leaves us hanging. It is your quiet time now. Amen.*

Say xanthomatous, say xenurine, say them over and over! Auntie Mary breaks the serrated silence. She pushes the skin under her right eye to stop it twitching. She knows today is the day (there is no day designated for celebrating the letter X, so today is as good as any). She doesn't want me to finish this book. I know how she feels.

Goodbyes are hard. 'Someday' has been my go-to reply when anyone asks are you there yet? There—where, exactly? I've lived too long with a case of the somedays. I remember Mum telling Brother BJ and me there's no need to be scared when things end, that our farm won't ever leave our bodies, and that someday we'll understand.

Then, an olive branch: It's not an end or even 'the end,' I tell Auntie Mary. Nothing ends because there's always a thing of sorts, even in the quietest, darkest, coldest, farthest out-there galaxy-blue places. It's why we can't predict a when for the end of time, find the end of the rainbow, cure longing, or 'be' at the end of any road. Longing is the longest road of all because it ends at Never Town. Even as the TOWN LIMITS sign shrinks in the rearview mirror, as the day's curtain sets on the horizon, The End always starts a new nothing.

Dad turns to salt. Mum sees through my grasping-at-straws out-of-breath blue. You look tired, sweetie, she says, her own eyes heavy. You should get that night-light program for your computer to lower the blue light from the screen. What color blue is that? I can only think of it as a tacit, tongue-tied blue.

Dad sniffs and gets up from the table to do 'something.' He will die walking in and out of Mum's kitchen.

Cup of tea? Mum offers.

Today, everything exists to end in a photograph, wrote Susan Sontag in *On Photography*. Pictures can tell us a story that words cannot, and vice versa. The word *farm* is in the syntax, fff-arm in contrast to disarm, which means to make safe, to win over. Our farm, my safelight. I have tried, I'm still trying, to build a wordless, light-filled place, a single photograph, for our farm to live safely and eternally. Somewhere far removed from the archive box, a place that cannot be packed, unpacked, and repacked. Oh, the folly of ownership, of thinking there is a 'forever home' outside of what is, when all is said and done, a box. Of my name, lover of home, the preamble to my story so far, oh, so far.

Bodies carry stories, and every story has risks, barriers, or disruptions. There are bolt-from-the-blue side effects from obsessing over something unknown. In the British sci-fi horror film *The Strange World of Planet X*, the unknown is conducting experiments about magnetic fields. For me, it's the push/pull of a past that refuses to pass and fields so magnetic that I'm forever stuck in place: I, a seed, rooted and firm. No photograph can unearth me.

———

Walking into nowhere is what I do when looking at a photograph. It is also where I mentally go when I take a picture. I make decisions, this location, not that. The world slow-dissolves behind me and beside me. Only what is frontal solidifies, and even then, details bleed. When I point my camera at the thing I'm attracted to, I birth an unreal world. My mind and the camera evolve it. When I take the camera away from my eye, I'm a runaway racehorse, sweating, panting, and wild into nowhere. My camera and I belong nowhere, have never belonged anywhere, not where I was born and raised, not in the rectangles in which flesh and paper versions of me live. I like photographing in nowhere because no one tells me I'm doing it wrong. No one cares if I have a camera. I can look any way I want. There are no catcalls or suspicious looks. Nowhere is where I fit in. Nowhere is where I go when I go back because I can't ever be back. The place I love isn't there anymore; it's nowhere, a kingdom all its own. And the only thing that marks the spot of my walking into nowhere is nothing. In nowhere, I'm a good kind of no one, nameless and alone.

'No one is special. But everyone can become special if the right eyes are looking your way': from the film *Toscana*, about what is left unsaid, if all our blank spaces stay unfilled.

I don't want to die nameless and alone, said Mr. X on the radio in 1939, a man who had lost his memory for eight years, living at the Mississippi State Hospital until he was identified following several public appeals.

What kind of happy ending are you looking for? Nan. E. gives a final bang on her coffin.

A part of me wants to tie all these musings in a bow and put it under the Xmas tree. There, job done, X1 credit card maxed out. Another part of me thinks about all those nice cups of tea, and why doesn't Mum say, *let's have a shitty lukewarm cup of that home-brand crap.* Well, crap, maybe I have to accept that my home is my body, that if I made a self-portrait right now, it would reveal only the scaffolding of a 'somebody' under construction where little photo ghosts work but have no intention of ever finishing. I have said the things I wanted to say that could only come from me. All the other parts of me, shreds really, have no idea what last words one might say about the letter X, photography, the battle to understand myself, and that one road in and out.

I tell my family: it's time to go home.

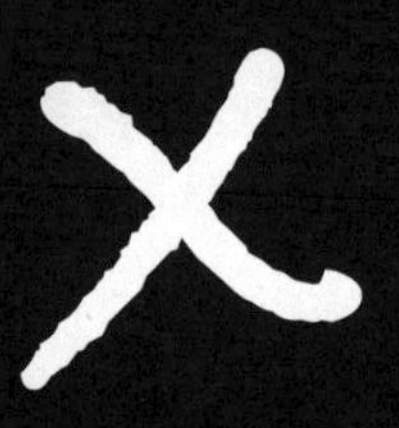

When you research or ask questions about a thing, it suddenly seems to appear everywhere, making you wonder how you didn't notice it before. You'll know what I mean if you've had your fortune told, your palms or tea leaves read, and the psychic says you'll see two birds, which mean this, that, the other. On your way home, presto! Two birds appear. Then another two. And another two. You start to worry. You're unsure which pair of birds is the right one to pay attention to. You begin to think about coincidences and irony in new ways. You consider fatalism. What if you had chosen a different 'thing' to focus on? Are you missing out because you're so fixated on this one thing that you're losing sight of that other thing?

This is what it has felt like to choose the letter X as the focus for this book. The letter X plus photography plus farm life, equals this: a blend of facts and family fallacies that swoop across pages like magpies. Even years after sitting at my desk to start writing, I can't unsee the X; it's imprinted on my retinas. Me: Look, there's an X! Family and friends: Aren't you done?

I could have chosen any set of three topics for this book, using autobiography as a foundation. We all have unique upbringings where signs repeat and overlap. Whether or not we notice them is another matter, another story for another time. The photographer Lisette Model once said that science, medicine, space, ESP, for peace, against peace, entertainment, television, and films cannot be found without photography. This seems true of the letter X, too. It has too much in common with photography and farm life for me to ignore. Plenty of subtext and secondary characters exist—religion, color, reproductive labor, and death. That last one—death—is also our common denominator in life. What's that saying about the only two guarantees in life being death and taxes? To those, I would add photographs.

While writing this book, I received many emails, texts, photographs, and letters: for your X book, about X, do you know this X, here's another X. Each of these X's bears the mark of its author. I am thankful to them and to friends who read early drafts: Thomas Barrow, Kim Beil, Cara Buzzell, Dan Boardman, Brown University Department of Visual Art, the Center for Creative Photography at the University of Arizona, Kelli Connell, Marc Elliott, Dan Estabrook, Ann Fessler, Nelis Franken, Jennifer Garza-Cuen, Hamidah Glasgow, Meggan Gould, Marvin Heiferman, Alan Huck, Angela Kelly, David Maisel, Owen McCarter, Aspen Mayes, Alison Nordstrom, Louie Palu, Ahndraya Parlato, Janet Pritchard, Macushla Robinson, Maarten Schilt, Emily Shapiro, Brea Souders, Gordon Stettinius, and Greg Stoodley.

Thank you, Mike Slack and Tricia Gabriel at The Ice Plant, for your creativity, kindness, and faith.

This story isn't mine alone. Whatever my writing offers stems from the points it shares with others, especially my family.

If X is to mark a spot for me, it is the place of a generous community that transcends biology, geography, and time. That place, that X, is the home I love most.

ISN'T X BEAUTIFUL!
© 2026 Odette Elix England for the text & images
© 2026 The Ice Plant for this edition

Edited & designed by Mike Slack & Tricia Gabriel
Coördination: Jacques Marlow

Distribution:
USA, UK, EU: artbook.com
France & Belgium: interart.fr
Asia: twelvebooks.co.jp
Australia & New Zealand: perimeterdistribution.co.au

Printed in Italy by Grafiche Veneziane Società Cooperativa

First printing, January 2026
ISBN 979-8-9857330-6-8

THE ICE PLANT
PO Box 29247, Los Angeles, CA 90029 • theiceplant.cc

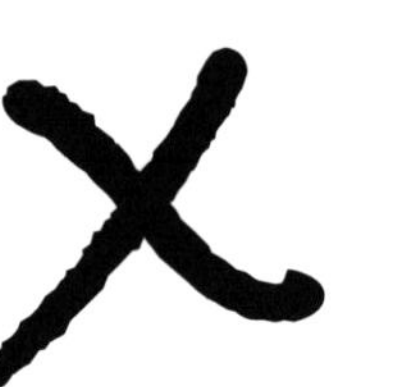